**New Directions for
Teaching and Learning**

Marilla D. Svinicki
EDITOR-IN-CHIEF

Team-Based Learning: Small-Group Learning's Next Big Step

Larry K. Michaelsen
Michael Sweet
Dean X. Parmelee
EDITORS

Number 116 • Winter 2008
Jossey-Bass
San Francisco

TEAM-BASED LEARNING: SMALL-GROUP LEARNING'S NEXT BIG STEP
Larry K. Michaelsen, Michael Sweet, Dean X. Parmelee (eds.)
New Directions for Teaching and Learning, no. 116
Marilla D. Svinicki, Editor-in-Chief

Microfilm copies of issues and articles are available in 16mm and 35mm, as well as microfiche in 105mm, through University Microfilms, Inc., 300 North Zeeb Road, Ann Arbor, Michigan 48106-1346.

NEW DIRECTIONS FOR TEACHING AND LEARNING (ISSN 0271-0633, electronic ISSN 1536-0768) is part of The Jossey-Bass Higher and Adult Education Series and is published quarterly by Wiley Subscription Services, Inc., A Wiley Company, at Jossey-Bass, 989 Market Street, San Francisco, California 94103-1741. Periodicals postage paid at San Francisco, California, and at additional mailing offices. POSTMASTER: Send address changes to New Directions for Teaching and Learning, Jossey-Bass, 989 Market Street, San Francisco, California 94103-1741.

New Directions for Teaching and Learning is indexed in CIJE: Current Index to Journals in Education (ERIC), Contents Pages in Education (T&F), Current Abstracts (EBSCO), Educational Research Abstracts Online (T&F), ERIC Database (Education Resources Information Center), Higher Education Abstracts (Claremont Graduate University), and SCOPUS (Elsevier).

SUBSCRIPTIONS cost $89 for individuals and $228 for institutions, agencies, and libraries in the United States. Prices subject to change. See order form at end of book.

EDITORIAL CORRESPONDENCE should be sent to the editor-in-chief, Marilla D. Svinicki, Department of Educational Psychology, University of Texas at Austin, One University Station, D5800, Austin, TX 78712.

www.josseybass.com

ISBN: 978-0-470-46212-6

Contents

PREFACE

Until the first book on team-based learning (TBL) was published in 2002 (Michaelsen, Knight, and Fink, 2002), this unique and powerful strategy was often seen as nothing more than another variant of cooperative learning, even though Michaelsen and a number of other faculty had been using, researching, and publishing about TBL since the late 1970s. In 2004 a slightly updated paperback version was published (Michaelsen, Knight, and Fink, 2004) in the more appropriate format as a trade book (rather than a reference book), with a more readable font and a more affordable price. As a result, the paperback quickly became the more commonly used version of the book. It has made TBL more visible to a wider range of audiences and has expanded its use to hundreds of disciplines and thousands of schools in at least twenty-three countries.

The question now, a half-decade later, is, "What else have we learned about TBL?" The answer is, "A great deal!" Although the essential elements of TBL have remained stable, more faculty have used TBL in a wider variety of disciplines, with a wider variety of student populations, and in a wider variety of educational settings. These efforts have resulted in a clearer understanding of what it takes to capture and retain the unusual educational power of TBL and avoid practices that can limit its effectiveness.

We begin this volume with a few cautionary tales about what TBL is not, then discuss briefly the new settings in which TBL is being implemented, and finally introduce the chapters that follow.

Treatment Fidelity: Cautionary Tales About What Team-Based Learning Is Not

When a new idea comes along that promises significantly better results than current practices, at least two problems can arise. The first is that people try only some parts of the idea. The second is that people do not heed best-practice advice about what is required to implement the process for success. The danger is that those who fall into either of these traps can conclude and tell others, "I tried this idea, and it did not work." Both kinds of problems have been reported to us, and as a result, we believe that a major contribution of this volume is informing potential users what they need to do—if they in fact want to *do* TBL and enjoy the significant benefits it has to offer.

This volume is about what TBL is and how it works, from the first chapter on the essential elements of team-based learning all the way through the key teaching activities in the appendix. (In fact, we generated the list in

NEW DIRECTIONS FOR TEACHING AND LEARNING, no. 116, Winter 2008   © Wiley Periodicals, Inc.
Published online in Wiley InterScience (www.interscience.wiley.com) • DOI: 10.1002/tl.329

the appendix after reflecting on reports we received of both kinds of problems described above.) We begin, however, with a consideration of what TBL is not.

When is a perceived implementation of TBL not really an implementation of TBL? To clarify this, we will describe some of the versions of TBL we have heard about that did not work, how it was a departure from TBL best practice, and explain why we believe the teacher experienced the results reported. (For readers who are new to TBL and not yet familiar with its terminology, a firm grasp of this concept is not necessary for the broad points we are making here.)

- *If you overuse readiness assurance tests, it is not TBL.* An example of the first problem with TBL is when professors become attracted to the ability of the readiness assurance tests (RATs) to motivate students to complete assigned readings but fail to use assignments that require students to apply the knowledge they acquire from those readings and RATs. When this happens, students wind up taking RATs followed by even more RATs. Then they complain about the process because the course has been transformed into a pattern of test after test after test and they feel cheated (we believe legitimately so) by being "rewarded" for memorizing meaningless detail followed by being expected to memorize even more meaningless detail.
- *Without peer evaluation, it is not TBL.* One respected psychology professor used readiness assurance tests and at least some application problems, but contrary to best practice, did not use also use student peer evaluations. The result? Although two of his three groups worked well and most students were very positive about their experience, one of the best students made the predictable (and valid) complaint: "I did most the work, and everyone in my group got the same credit. This is not fair." Unfortunately, this professor concluded that TBL "did not work for good students in his discipline," and in spite of numerous and well-publicized successes with TBL elsewhere on campus, it was over twenty years before anyone in his psychology department experimented with TBL again.
- *If you do not properly introduce your students to TBL, they will likely perceive it as an alien way of teaching and will resist it.* Sometimes a teacher implements the entire TBL system and is gratified to see students engaged in significant learning, but is then frustrated by surprisingly low course evaluations at the end of the term. In our experience, this occurs because the professor has, contrary to good practice, failed to spend time at the outset explaining what TBL is, why the course is being taught with it, identifying its benefits, and providing an early, nongraded practice exercise to let students experience for themselves the uniqueness and potential benefits of the process. Often these teachers simply announce that they will be using TBL and warn students, with a minimum of explanation, that they need to start studying because the next class will start with a readiness assurance test. This can make students feel confused, unsafe,

and perhaps even a little ambushed. As a result, in spite of the positive evidence of improved student learning in TBL classrooms, some professors (and we suspect many of their peers) have come to view TBL as being a potential career risk.

These are just some examples of teachers not following best practice and attributing many of the resulting problems on TBL as a teaching method. Unfortunately, the stories these teachers then tell can prevent others from trying TBL for themselves and discovering what it really does have to offer. We are aware of at least one instance in which, contrary to Michaelsen's repeated warning that lengthy group papers are the worst type of group assignment, one of our colleagues said to the class, "Because of Michaelsen's success with TBL, I've decided to try it out this semester. So form your own groups, and pick a topic for a thirty-page term paper that will be due on the Friday before finals." Results? The better students complained because the less responsible students did little or nothing; the professor concluded that TBL did not work in his subject area; and the majority of the students (who had not actually experienced TBL) concluded that TBL was a bad idea.

Expanded Use of Team-Based Learning

The publication of the original books on TBL in 2002 and 2004 led to much greater awareness and use of TBL, making the publication of this volume a timely update on current practice. Three areas in which this expanded use has been especially noteworthy are in professional education (the health professions and engineering, for example), internationally, and in mixed-mode and online environments.

TBL in Professional Schools. Professional school educators have found TBL particularly attractive because it offers powerful solutions to several major problems they face:

- The need for students to acquire and retain what seems to be an increasingly large volume of content knowledge and the ability to use that content to solve the problems that occur in students' future professional practice
- The need for students to develop a sophisticated level of interpersonal skills so that they can work effectively as members of interdisciplinary groups and teams
- Frequently having to teach in large-class settings

Consequently professional educators have organized several initiatives:

- The publication of a book for health professions educators (Michaelsen, Parmalee, Levine, and McMahon, 2008) in which the authors describe their use of TBL with different kinds of subject matter and in different settings

- Several Web sites on using TBL in professional schools (for example, in business, engineering, and health professions)
- A password-protected repository for sharing teaching modules for the health professions
- An annual conference on using TBL in the health professions

TBL in International Settings. Another exciting area in which TBL has grown is in international contexts. Based on personal contact with the authors of this volume and our awareness with professional publications, TBL is now being used in at least twenty-three countries outside the United States and on every continent. Furthermore, due in part to the impact of the Internet, we are regularly asked to present workshops on TBL at schools virtually worldwide. As a result, many of the chapters in this volume examine how and why TBL enables students to learn to work in diverse teams and to value differing opinions and why TBL is effective in such a wide variety of cultural settings.

TBL and Instructional Technology. Instructional technology is increasingly affecting every aspect of higher education, including the use of TBL in various forms of technology-mediated instruction. As a result, two of the chapters specifically focus on technological innovations that have been applied to TBL. One outlines a number of ideas for using technology to enhance face-to-face implementations of TBL. The other describes two authors' experiences with implementing TBL in a totally asynchronous, online environment.

Organization of this Volume

This volume is designed to address three questions:

- What are the essential elements of TBL?
- Why are these elements essential to TBL?
- What do faculty members need to do to implement these essential elements in a variety of different contexts?

These three questions are addressed in the following chapters.

In Chapter One, Michaelsen and Sweet outline the specifics of what needs to happen for someone to accurately say, "I used TBL." In Chapter Two, Sweet and Pelton-Sweet use transcripts of student interactions to show how and why the readiness assurance process has such a powerful and positive effect on the development of lasting and productive interpersonal relationships within teams.

In Chapter Three, Sibley and Parmelee outline why TBL is ideally suited for dealing with the challenges of the professional school curriculum and describe, through the eyes and voices of students, what it is like to be in a professional school TBL course.

NEW DIRECTIONS FOR TEACHING AND LEARNING • DOI: 10.1002/tl

In Chapter Four, Lane discusses why facilitation skills are so important in TBL and provides concrete facilitation tools and suggestions, as well as describing certain teacher characteristics that can make TBL easier or more difficult to implement successfully.

Then in Chapter Five, Cestone, Levine, and Lane outline why peer evaluations are such an important part of TBL and describe a variety of options for collecting peer assessment data and providing formative and summative feedback to students.

The final two chapters deal with the impact of technology on TBL. In Chapter Six, Robinson and Walker outline a number of technical enhancement options for implementing TBL in face-to-face classes. Finally, in Chapter Seven, Palsolé and Awalt describe how they have successfully implemented TBL in purely asynchronous, online environments.

TBL Through the Eyes of Students

We have recognized for some time that TBL is about learning, not teaching. But in part because of the more widespread use of TBL, we have only recently realized the value of inviting the voices of students into the scholarly and practical conversations about TBL. As a result, a major feature of several chapters in this volume is that they reinforce many of TBL's key ideas by using the very words of students who have experienced and are experiencing TBL.

Larry K. Michaelsen
L. Dee Fink
Editors

References

Michaelsen, L. K., Knight, A. B., and Fink, L. D. *Team-Based Learning: A Transformative Use of Small Groups in College Teaching.* Sterling, Va.: Stylus, 2004.

Michaelsen, L. K., Knight, A. B., and Fink, L. D. *Team-Based Learning: A Transformative Use of Small Groups in College Teaching.* Westport, Conn.: Praeger, 2002.

Michaelsen, L. K., Parmelee, D. X., McMahon, K. K., & Levine, R. E. (Eds.). *Team-Based Learning for Health Professions Education: A Guide to Using Small Groups for Improving Learning.* Sterling, VA: Stylus, 2008.

LARRY K. MICHAELSEN *is professor of management at Central Missouri, David Ross Boyd Professor Emeritus at the University of Oklahoma, a Carnegie Scholar, and former editor of the Journal of Management Education.*

L. DEE FINK *was director of the Instructional Development Program at the University of Oklahoma from 1979 until 2005 and currently is a national and international consultant in higher education.*

TBL is a collection of practices that support one another for powerful instructional effect. This chapter describes the building blocks of team-based learning and the steps necessary to put them into place.

The Essential Elements of Team-Based Learning

Larry K. Michaelsen, Michael Sweet

Team-based learning (TBL) possibly relies on small group interaction more heavily than any other commonly used instructional strategy in postsecondary education (for comparative discussion of different approaches, see Fink, 2004; Johnson, Johnson, and Smith, 2007; Millis and Cottell, 1998). This conclusion is based on three facts. First, with TBL, group work is central to exposing students to and improving their ability to apply course content. Second, with TBL, the vast majority of class time is used for group work. Third, courses taught with TBL typically involve multiple group assignments that are designed to improve learning and promote the development of self-managed learning teams.

This chapter begins with a brief overview of TBL. Next, we discuss the four essential elements of TBL and then walk through the steps required to implement them. Finally, we examine some of the benefits that students, administrators, and faculty can expect from a successful implementation of TBL.

A Broad Overview of TBL

The primary learning objective in TBL is to go beyond simply covering content and focus on ensuring that students have the opportunity to practice using course concepts to solve problems. Thus, TBL is designed to provide students with both conceptual and procedural knowledge. Although some time in the TBL classroom is spent ensuring that students master the course

NEW DIRECTIONS FOR TEACHING AND LEARNING, no. 116, Winter 2008 © Wiley Periodicals, Inc.
Published online in Wiley InterScience (www.interscience.wiley.com) • DOI: 10.1002/tl.330

content, the vast majority of class time is used for team assignments that focus on using course content to solve the kinds of problems that students are likely to face in the future. Figure 1.1 outlines generally how time in one unit of a TBL course is organized.

In a TBL course, students are strategically organized into permanent groups for the term, and the course content is organized into major units—typically five to seven. Before any in-class content work, students must study assigned materials because each unit begins with the readiness assurance process (RAP). The RAP consists of a short test on the key ideas from the readings that students complete as individuals; then they take the same test again as a team, coming to consensus on team answers. Students receive immediate feedback on the team test and then have the opportunity to write evidence-based appeals if they feel they can make valid arguments for their answer to questions that they got wrong. The final step in the RAP is a lecture (usually very short and always very specific) to enable the instructor to clarify any misperceptions that become apparent during the team test and the appeals.

Once the RAP is completed, the remainder (and the majority) of the learning unit is spent on in-class activities and assignments that require students to practice using the course content.

The Four Essential Elements of Team-Based Learning

Shifting from simply familiarizing students with course concepts to requiring that students use those concepts to solve problems is no small task. Making this shift requires changes in the roles of both instructor and students. The instructor's primary role shifts from dispensing information to designing and managing the overall instructional process, and the students' role shifts from being passive recipients of information to one of accepting responsibility for the initial exposure to the course content so that they will be prepared for the in-class teamwork.

Changes of this magnitude do not happen automatically and may even seem to be a dream rather than an achievable reality. They are, however, achievable when the four essential elements of TBL are successfully implemented:

- Groups. Groups must be properly formed and managed.
- Accountability. Students must be accountable for the quality of their individual and group work.
- Feedback. Students must receive frequent and timely feedback.
- Assignment design. Group assignments must promote both learning and team development.

When these four elements are implemented in a course, the stage is set for student groups to evolve into cohesive learning teams.

Figure 1.1. Team-Based Instructional Activity Sequence

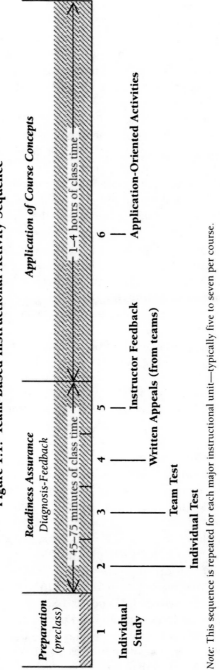

Note: This sequence is repeated for each major instructional unit—typically five to seven per course.

Element 1: Properly Formed and Managed Groups. TBL requires that the instructor oversee the formation of the groups so that he or she can manage three important variables: ensuring that the groups have adequate resources to draw from in completing their assignments and approximately the same level of those resources across groups, avoiding membership coalitions that are likely to interfere with the development of group cohesiveness, and ensuring that groups have the opportunity to develop into learning teams.

Distributing Member Resources. In order for groups to function as effectively as possible, they should be as diverse as possible. Each group should contain a mix of student characteristics that might make the course easier or more difficult for a student to do well in the course (for example, previous course work or course-related practical experience) as well as demographic characteristics like gender and ethnicity. The goal here is to equip groups to succeed by populating them with members who will bring different perspectives to the task.

Findings in both group dynamics research (Brobeck and others, 2002) and educational research (Chan, Burtis, and Bereiter, 1997) illuminate the positive impact of diverse input in problem-solving discussions on both learning and performance. When group members bring many different perspectives to a task, their process of collaborative knowledge building in pursuit of consensus is powerful to watch. In addition, although member diversity initially inhibits both group processes and performance, it is likely to become an asset when members have worked together over time and under conditions that promote group cohesiveness (Watson, Kumar, and Michaelsen, 1993).

Minimizing Barriers to Group Cohesiveness: Avoiding Coalitions. Coalitions within a group are likely to threaten its overall development. In newly formed groups, either a previously established relationship between a subset of members in the group (such as a boyfriend and girlfriend or fraternity brothers) or the potential for a cohesive subgroup based on background factors such as nationality, culture, or native language is likely to burden a group with insider-outsider tension that can plague the group throughout the term. Because it is human nature to seek out similar others, allowing students free rein in forming their own groups practically ensures the existence of potentially disruptive subgroups (Fiechtner and Davis, 1985; Michaelsen and Black, 1994).

Time. Any group dynamics textbook will tell you that groups need time to develop into high-performing teams, regardless of whether you favor sequential or life cycle models (Tuckman, 1965; Tuckman and Jensen, 1977), cyclical models (Worchel, Wood, and Simpson, 1992), or adaptive or nonsequential models (McGrath, 1991). For this reason, students should stay in the same group for the entire course. Although even a single well-designed group assignment usually produces a variety of positive outcomes, only when students work together over time can their groups become cohesive enough to evolve into self-managed and truly effective learning teams.

NEW DIRECTIONS FOR TEACHING AND LEARNING • DOI: 10.1002/tl

Element 2: Student Accountability for Individual and Group Work. In lecture classes, there is no need for students to be accountable to anyone other than the instructor. By contrast, TBL requires students to be accountable to both the instructor and their teammates for the quality and quantity of their individual work. Furthermore, teams must accountable for the quality and quantity of their work as a unit. (For a review of the effects of accountability on an array of social judgments and choices, see Lerner and Tetlock, 1999.)

Accountability for Individual Preclass Preparation. Lack of preparation places clear limits on both individual learning and team development. If several members of a team come unprepared to contribute to a complex group task, then the team as a whole is far less likely to succeed at that task, cheating its members of the learning that the task was designed to stimulate. No amount of discussion can overcome absolute ignorance. Furthermore, lack of preparation also hinders the development of cohesiveness because those who do make the effort to be prepared will resent having to carry their peers. As a result, the effective use of learning groups clearly requires that individual students be made accountable for class preparation.

Accountability for Contributing to The Team. The next step is ensuring that members contribute time and effort to group work. In order to accurately assess members' contributions to the success of their teams, it is imperative that instructors involve the students themselves in a peer assessment process. That is, members should be given the opportunity to evaluate one another's contributions to the activities of the team. Contributions to the team include activities such as individual preparation for teamwork, reliable class attendance, attendance at team meetings that may have occurred outside class, positive contributions to team discussions, and valuing and encouraging contributions from fellow team members. Peer assessment is essential because team members are typically the only ones who have enough information to evaluate one another's contributions accurately.

Accountability for High-Quality Team Performance. The third significant factor in ensuring accountability is developing an effective means to assess team performance. There are two keys to effectively assessing teams. One is using assignments that require teams to create a product that can be readily compared across teams and with "expert" opinions, and the other is using procedures to ensure that such comparisons occur frequently and in a timely manner.

Element 3: Frequent Immediate Student Feedback. Immediate feedback is the primary instructional lever in TBL for two very different reasons. First, feedback is essential to content learning and retention—a notion that not only makes intuitive sense but is also well documented in educational research literature (Bruning, Schraw, and Ronning, 1994; Kulik and Kulik, 1988; Hattie and Timperley, 2007). Second, immediate feedback has tremendous impact on group development (for a review, see Birmingham and McCord, 2004).

NEW DIRECTIONS FOR TEACHING AND LEARNING • DOI: 10.1002/tl

Element 4: Assignments That Promote Both Learning and Team Development. The most fundamental aspect of designing team assignments that promote both learning and team development is ensuring that they truly require group interaction. In most cases, team assignments generate a high level of interaction if they require teams to use course concepts to make decisions that involve a complex set of issues and enable teams to report their decisions in a simple form. When assignments emphasize making decisions, most students choose to complete the task by engaging each other in a give-and-take content-related discussion. By contrast, assignments that involve producing complex output such as a lengthy document often limit both learning and team development because they typically inhibit intrateam discussions in two ways. First, discussions are likely to be much shorter because students are likely to feel an urgency to create the product that is to be graded. Second, instead of focusing on content-related issues, they are likely to center on how to divide up the work. Thus, complex product outputs such as a lengthy document seldom contribute to team development because they are likely to have been created by individual members working alone on their part of the overall project.

Summary. By adhering to the four essential elements of TBL—careful design of groups, accountability, feedback, and assignments—teachers create a context that promotes the quantity and quality of interaction required to transform groups into highly effective learning teams. Appropriately forming the teams puts them on equal footing and greatly reduces the possibility of mistrust from preexisting relationships between a subset of team members. Holding students accountable for preparation and attendance motivates team members to behave in prosocial ways that build cohesiveness and foster trust. Using RAPs and other assignments to provide ongoing and timely feedback on both individual and team performance enables teams to develop confidence in their ability to capture the intellectual resources of all their members. Assignments that promote both learning and team development motivate members to challenge others' ideas for the good of the team. Also, over time, students' confidence in their teams grows to the point that they are willing and able to tackle difficult assignments with little or no external help.

Implementing Team-Based Learning

Effectively using TBL typically requires redesigning a course from beginning to end, and the redesign process should begin well before the start of the school term. The process involves making decisions about and designing activities at four different times: before class begins, the first day of class, each major unit of instruction, and near the end of the course. In this section, we discuss the practical steps a TBL instructor takes at each of these points, but for a treatment that is even detailed and practical, we direct readers to Michaelsen, Knight, and Fink (2004).

Before Class Begins. Traditional education, particularly in undergraduate programs, has tended to separate knowledge acquisition from knowledge application both between and within courses. In a typical biology course, for example, students listen to lectures through which they are expected to absorb a great deal of knowledge that they will then later be asked to put to use in a biology lab. In fact, even within higher-level courses, students often spend much of the term absorbing knowledge that they do not put to use until a project that is due just prior to the final exam.

TBL uses a fundamentally different knowledge acquisition and knowledge application model. With TBL, students repeat the knowledge acquisition and knowledge application cycle several times within each individual course. They individually study the course content, discuss it with their peers and the instructor, and immediately apply it in making choices that require them to use their knowledge. Thus, students in TBL courses develop a much better sense of the relevance of the material because they seldom have to make unreasonably large inferences about when and how the content might become useful in the real world. Rather than being filled with libraries of "inert knowledge" (Whitehead, 1929), from which they then later must extract needed information with great effort, students walk away from TBL courses having already begun the practical problem-solving process of learning to use their knowledge in context.

This benefit, however, does not occur by accident. Designing a successful TBL course involves making decisions related to first identifying and clustering instructional objectives and then designing a grading system around them.

Identifying Instructional Objectives. Designing a TBL course requires instructors to "think backward." What is meant by "think backward"? In most forms of higher education, teachers design their courses by asking themselves what they feel students need to know, then telling the students that information, and finally testing the students on how well they absorbed what they were told. In contrast, designing a TBL course requires instructors to "think backward"—backward because they are planned around what they want students to be able to do when they have finished the course; only then do instructors think about what students need to know. Wiggins and McTighe (1998) used the term *backward design* to describe this method of course design, which enables the instructor to build a course that provides students both declarative and procedural knowledge (in other words, conceptual knowledge and the ability to use that knowledge in decision making). This is a useful distinction, but if you have taught only with conceptual familiarization as your goal, it can be surprisingly difficult to identify what exactly you want students to be able to do on completion of a course. The following question is a good a good place to start.

What are the students who really understand the material doing that shows you they get it? Imagine you are working shoulder-to-shoulder with a former student who is now a junior colleague. In a wonderful moment, you see that colleague do something that makes you think, "Hey! She really got from my class what I wanted her to get. There's the evidence right there!" When you are designing a course backward, the question you ask yourself is: "What specifically is that evidence? What could a former student be doing in a moment like that to make it obvious she really internalized what you were trying to teach her and is putting it to use in a meaningful way?"

For every course, there are several answers to this question, and these different answers correspond to the units of the redesigned version of the course. A given real-world moment will likely demand knowledge from one part of a course but not another, so for any given course, you should brainstorm about a half-dozen of these proud moments in which a former student is making it obvious that she really learned what you wanted her to. For now, do not think about the classroom; just imagine she is doing something in an actual organizational context. Also, do not be afraid to get too detailed as you visualize these moments. In fact, come up with as many details as you can about how this former student is doing what she is doing, what decisions she is making, in what sequence, under what conditions, and so on.

These detailed scenarios become useful in three ways. First, the actions taking place in the scenarios will help you organize your course into units. Second, the scenarios will enable you to use class time to build students' applied knowledge instead of inert knowledge. Third, the details of the scenario will help you design the criteria for the assessments on which you can base students' grades.

Once you have brainstormed the scenarios and the details that accompany them, you have identified your instructional objectives, which often involve making decisions that are based on insightful applications of the concepts from your course. Now you are ready to ask three more questions:

- *What will students need to know in order to be able to do those things?* Answers to this question will guide your selection of a textbook, the contents of your course packet, experiential exercises, and are likely to prompt you to provide supplementary materials of your own creation or simple reading guides to help students focus on what you consider most important in the readings or lab findings. In addition, the answers will be key in developing questions for the readiness assurance process.
- *While solving problems, what knowledge will students need to make decisions?* Answers to this question will help you import the use of course knowledge from your brainstormed real-world scenarios into the classroom. You may not be able to bring the actual organizational settings in which your scenarios occurred into the classroom, although computer simulations, video (including full-length feature films), and requiring students to learn by doing (see Miller, 1991, and Michaelsen and McCord, 2006) are coming much closer to approaching the real world. But you can provide enough relevant information about those settings to design

activities that require students to face the same kinds of problems and make the same kinds of decisions they will make in clinical and laboratory settings.

- *What criteria separate a well-made decision from a poorly made decision using this knowledge?* Answers to this question will help you begin building the measures you will use to determine how well the students have learned the material and how well they can put it to use under specific conditions.

In summary, TBL leverages the power of action-based instructional objectives to not only expose students to course content but also give them practice using it. When you are determining an instructional objective, it is crucial to know how to assess the extent to which students have mastered that objective. Some teachers feel that designing assessments first removes something from the value of instruction—that it simply becomes teaching to the test. With TBL the view is that you should teach to the test as long as the test represents (as closely as possible) the real use to which students will ultimately apply the course material: what they are going to do with it, not just what they should know about it.

Designing a Grading System. The other step in redesigning the course is to ensure that the grading system is designed to reward the right things. An effective grading system for TBL must provide incentives for individual contributions and effective work by the teams, as well as address the equity concerns that naturally arise when group work is part of an individual's grade. The primary concern here is typically borne from past group work situations in which students were saddled with free-riding team members and have resented it ever since. Students worry that they will be forced to choose between getting a low grade or carrying their less able or less motivated peers. Instructors worry that they will have to choose between grading rigorously and grading fairly.

Fortunately, many of these concerns are alleviated by a grading system in which a significant proportion of the grade is based on individual performance, team performance, and each member's contributions to the success of the teams. As long as that standard is met, the primary remaining concern is that the relative weight of the factors is acceptable to both the instructor and the students.

The First Day of Class. Activities that occur during the first few hours of class are critical to the success of TBL. During that time, the teacher must accomplish four objectives: ensure that students understand why you (the instructor) have decided to use TBL and what that means about the way the class will be conducted, form the groups, alleviate students' concerns about the grading system, and set up mechanisms to encourage the development of positive group norms.

Introducing Students to TBL. Because the roles of instructor and students are so fundamentally different from traditional instructional practice, it is critical that students understand both the rationale for using TBL and what that means about the way the class will be conducted. Educating students about TBL requires at a minimum providing them with an overview of the basic features of TBL, how TBL affects the role of the instructor and their role as students, and why they are likely to benefit from their experience in the course. This information should be printed in the course syllabus, presented orally, and demonstrated by one or more activities.

In order to foster students' understanding of TBL, we recommend two activities. The first is to explain the basic features of TBL using overhead transparencies (or a PowerPoint presentation) and clearly spelling out how the learning objectives for the course will be accomplished through the use of TBL, compared to how the same objectives would be achieved using a lecture-discussion course format. The second activity is a demonstration of a readiness assurance process using the course syllabus, a short reading on TBL, or some potentially useful ideas, such as what helps and hinders team development or strategies for giving helpful feedback (see Michaelsen and Schultheiss, 1988) as the content material to be covered. (In a class period of less than an hour, this activity might occur on day 2.)

Forming the Groups. When forming groups, you must consider the course-relevant characteristics of the students and the potential for the emergence of subgroups. As a result, the starting point in the group formation process is to gather information about specific student characteristics that will make it easier or more difficult for a student to succeed in the class. For a particular course, characteristics that could make it easier for a student to succeed might include previous relevant course work or practical experience or access to perspectives from other cultures. Most commonly, characteristics making it more difficult for students to succeed are the absence of those that would make it easier, but might include such things as a lack of language fluency.

We recommend forming the groups in class in the presence of the students to eliminate student concerns about ulterior motives the instructor may have had in forming groups. (For a depiction of how to form groups quickly and effectively, see Michaelsen and Sweet, 2008, and for a more detailed explanation and video demonstration, go to www.teambasedlearning.org.)

Alleviating Student Concerns About Grades. The next step in getting started on the right foot with TBL is to address student concerns about the grading system. Fortunately, student anxiety based on previous experience with divided-up group assignments largely evaporates as students come to understand two of the essential features of TBL. One is that two elements of the grading system create a high level of individual accountability for pre-class preparation, class attendance, and devoting time and energy to group assignments: counting individual scores on the readiness assurance tests and basing part of the grade on a peer evaluation. The other reassuring feature is that team assignments will be done in class and will be based on thinking, discussing, and deciding, so it is highly unlikely that one or two less-motivated teammates members can put the entire group at risk.

Many instructors choose to alleviate student concerns about grades by directly involving students in customizing the grading system to the class. Students become involved by participating in setting grade weights (Michaelsen, Cragin, and Watson, 1981; Michaelsen, Knight, and Fink, 2004). Within limits set by the instructor, representatives of the newly formed teams negotiate with one another to reach a consensus (all of the representatives must agree) on a mutually acceptable set of weights for each of the grade components: individual performance, team performance, and each member's contributions to the success of the team. After an agreement has been reached regarding the grade weight for each component, the standard applies for all groups for the remainder of the course.

Each Major Unit of Instruction. Each unit of a TBL course begins with a readiness assurance process (RAP), which occurs at least five to seven times each term. The RAP provides the foundation for individual and team accountability and has five major components: (1) assigned readings, (2) individual tests, (3) team tests, (4) an appeals process, and (5) instructor feedback.

Assigned Readings. Prior to the beginning of each major instructional unit, students are given reading and other assignments that should contain information on the concepts and ideas that must be understood to be able to solve the problem set out for this unit. Students complete the assignments and come to the next class period prepared to take a test on the assigned materials.

Individual Test. The first in-class activity in each instructional unit is an individual readiness assurance test (iRAT) over the material contained in the preclass assignments. The tests typically consist of multiple-choice questions that enable the instructor to assess whether students have a sound understanding of the key concepts from the readings. As a result, the questions should focus on foundational concepts, not picky details, and be difficult enough to stimulate team discussion.

Team Test. When students have finished the iRAT, they turn in their answers (which are often scored during the team test) and immediately proceed to the third phase of the readiness assurance process, the tRAT. During this third phase, students retake the same test, but this time as a team, and the teams must reach agreement on the answers to each test question. They then immediately check the correctness of their decision using the intermediate feedback assessment technique (IF-AT), a self-scoring answer sheet (see Figure 1.2) that provides feedback on each team decision. With the IF-AT answer sheets, students scratch off the covering of one of four (or five) boxes in search of a mark indicating they have found the correct answer. If they find the mark on the first try, they receive full credit. If not, they continue scratching until they find the mark, but their score is reduced with each unsuccessful scratch. This allows teams to receive partial credit for proximate knowledge.

The answer sheets are an effective way to provide timely feedback on the team RATs (not the iRATs—otherwise members would know the answers before the team test and discussion would be pointless). Furthermore, using

Figure 1.2. Immediate Feedback Assessment Technique

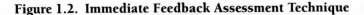

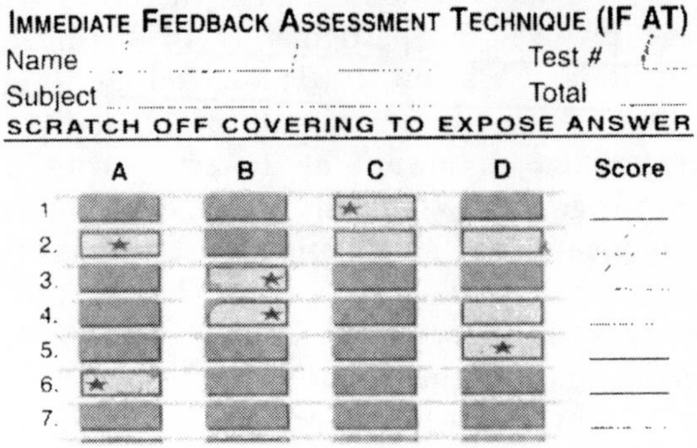

the answer sheets makes it possible to provide real-time content feedback to multiple teams without requiring them to maintain the same work pace.

Getting real-time feedback from the IF-AT provides two key benefits to the teams. First, it enables members to correct their misconceptions of the subject matter. Finding a star immediately after scratching the choice confirms the validity of it, and finding a blank box lets them know they have more work to do. Second, it promotes both the ability and the motivation for teams, with no input from the instructor, to learn how to work together effectively. In fact, those who have used the IF-ATs for their tRATs have learned that doing so virtually eliminates any possibility that one or two members might dominate team discussions. "Pushy" members are only one scratch away from embarrassing themselves, and quiet members are one scratch away from being validated as a valuable source of information and two scratches away from being told that they need to speak up.

The impact of the IF-AT on team development is immediate, powerful, and extremely positive. In our judgment, using the IF-ATs with the tRATs is the most effective tool available for promoting both concept understanding and cohesiveness in learning teams. Anyone who does not use them will miss a sure-fire way to implement TBL successfully.

Appeals Process. At this point in the readiness assurance process, students proceed to the fourth phase, which gives them the opportunity to refer to their assigned reading material and appeal any questions missed on the group test. That is, students are allowed to do a focused restudy of the assigned readings (this phase is "open book") to challenge the teacher about their responses on specific items on the team test or about confusion created by either the quality of the questions or inadequacies of the preclass readings.

Discussion among group members is usually very animated while the students work together to build a case to support their appeals. The students must produce compelling evidence to convince the teacher to award credit for the answers they missed. Teachers listening to students argue the fine details of course material while writing team appeals report being convinced their students learn more from appealing answers they got wrong than from confirming the answers they got right. As an integral part of the readiness assurance process, this appeals exercise provides yet another review of the readings.

Instructor Feedback. The fifth and final part of the readiness assurance process is oral feedback from the instructor. This feedback comes immediately after the appeals process and allows the instructor to clear up any confusion students may have about any of the concepts presented in the readings. As a result, input from the instructor is typically limited to a brief, focused review of only the most challenging aspects of the preclass reading assignment.

The Readiness Assurance Process in Summary. This process allows instructors to minimize class time that often is used instead to cover material that students can learn on their own. Time is saved because the instructor's input occurs after students have individually studied the material, taken an individual test focused on key concepts from the reading assignment, retaken the same test as a member of a learning team, and completed a focused restudy of the most difficult concepts. A cursory review of team test results illuminates for instructors which concepts need additional attention so that they can correct students' misunderstandings. In contrast to the concerns many instructors express about "losing time to group work" and not being able to cover as much content, many others report being able to cover more with the readiness assurance process than they can through lectures (Knight, 2004). Leveraging the motivational power and instructional efficiency of the readiness assurance process leaves the class a great deal of class time to develop students' higher-level learning skills as they tackle multiple and challenging application-oriented assignments.

Beyond its instructional power, the readiness assurance process is the backbone of TBL because it promotes team development in four specific ways. First, starting early in the course (usually the first few class hours), students are exposed to immediate and unambiguous feedback on both individual and team performance. As a result, each member is explicitly accountable for his or her preclass preparation. Second, because team members work face-to-face, the impact of the interaction is immediate and personal. Third, students have a strong vested interest in the outcome of the group and are motivated to engage in a high level of interaction. Finally, cohesiveness continues to build during the final stage of the process when the instructor is presenting information. This is because unlike lectures, the content of the instructor's comments is determined by students' choices and actions during the readiness tests. Thus, the instructor's comments provide either positive reinforcement (they celebrate together) or corrective instruction (which, particularly in the presence of other groups, can be experienced as embarrassing and, in this way, provide an "external threat" that builds cohesiveness within a group). Although the impact of the readiness assurance process on student learning is limited primarily to ensuring that they have a solid exposure to the content, it also increases students' ability to solve difficult problems for two reasons. First, by encouraging preclass preparation and a lively discussion, the process builds the intellectual competence of team members. Second, because they have immediate performance feedback, the experience of working together during the group and in preparing appeals heightens their ability and willingness to provide high-quality content feedback to one another. As a result, the readiness assurance process provides a practical way of ensuring that even in large classes, students are exposed to a high volume of immediate feedback that in some ways can actually be better than having a one-on-one relationship between student and instructor.

Promoting Higher-Level Learning. The final stage in the TBL instructional activity sequence for each unit of instruction is using one or more assignments that provide students with the opportunity to deepen their understanding by having groups use the concepts to solve a problem. These application assignments must foster both accountability and give-and-take discussion first within and then between groups. Designing these assignments is probably the most challenging aspect of implementing TBL.

The key to creating and implementing effective group assignments is following what TBL users fondly refer to as the 4 S's: (1) assignments should always be designed around a problem that is *significant to students,* (2) all of the students in the class should be working on the *same* problem, (3) students should be required to make a *specific* choice, and (4) groups should *simultaneously* report their choices (Figure 1.3). Furthermore, these procedures apply to all three stages in which students interface with course concepts—individual work prior to group discussions, discussions within groups, and whole-class discussion between groups. The 4 S's are explained in the following paragraphs.

Figure 1.3. Keys to Creating Effective Group Assignments

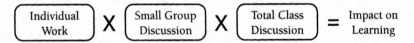

To obtain the maximum impact on learning, assignments at each stage should be characterized by 4 S's:

- **Significant** – Individuals and groups should work on a problem, case, or question demonstrating concept's usefulness.
- **Same problem** – Individuals and groups should work on the same problem, case, or question.
- **Specific choice** – Individuals and groups should be required to use course concepts to make a specific choice.
- **Simultaneously report** – If possible, individuals and groups should report their choices simultaneously.

- *Significant problem.* Effective assignments must capture students' interest. Unless assignments are built around what they see as a relevant issue, most students will view what they are being asked to do as busywork and will put forth the minimum effort required to get a satisfactory grade. The key to identifying what will be significant to students is using backward design. If you identify something you want students to be able to do and give them the chance to try, it is likely that your enthusiasm will carry over to your students in a way that rarely happens when you organize your teaching around what you think students should know.
- *Same problem.* Group assignments are effective only to the extent that they promote discussion both within and between groups. Assigning students to work on different problems practically eliminates meaningful discussions because students have little energy to engage in a comparison of apples and oranges, and students will not be exposed to feedback on the quality of their thinking as either individuals or teams. In order to facilitate a conceptually rich and energetic exchange, students must have a common frame of reference that is possible only when they are working on the same problem, that is, the same assignment or learning activity.
- *Specific choice.* Cognitive research shows that learning is greatly enhanced when students are required to engage in higher-level thinking (Mayer, 2002; Pintrich, 2002; Scandura, 1983). In order to challenge students to process information at higher levels of cognitive complexity, an educational adage (sometimes attributed to William Sparke) is that teaching consists of causing people to go into situations from which they cannot escape except by thinking.

In general, the best activity to accomplish this goal is to require students to make a specific choice. Think of the task of a courtroom jury: members are given complex information and asked to produce a simple decision: guilty or not guilty. As a result, nearly one hundred percent of their time and effort is spent digging into the details of their content. In the classroom, the best way to promote content-related discussion is to use assignments that require groups to use course concepts to make decisions on questions such as these:

- Which line on this tax form would pose the greatest financial risk due to an IRS audit? Why?
- Given a set of real data, which of the following advertising claims is least (or most) supportable? Why?
- What is the most dangerous aspect of this bridge design? Why?
- Given four short paragraphs, which is the best (or worst) example of an enthymeme? Why?

For a much more thorough discussion of assignments and a rationale as to why they work so well in promoting both student learning and team development, see Michaelsen, Knight, and Fink, 2004).

- *Simultaneous reports.* Once groups have made their choices, they can share the result of their thinking with the rest of the class sequentially or simultaneously. The problem with sequential reporting is that the initial response often has a powerful impact on the subsequent discussion because later-reporting teams tend to change their answer in response to what seems to be an emerging majority view—even if that majority is wrong.

This phenomenon, which we call answer drift, limits both learning and team development for a variety of reasons. One is that it is most likely to occur when the problems being discussed have the greatest potential for producing a meaningful discussion. That is because the more difficult or ambiguous the problem is, the greater the likelihood is that the initial response would be incomplete or even incorrect, and subsequent groups would be unsure about the correctness of their answer. Another is that answer drift discourages give-and-take discussions because later responders deliberately downplay differences between their initial answer and the one that is being discussed. Finally, sequential reporting limits accountability because the only group that is truly accountable is the one that opens the discussion.

Requiring groups to simultaneously reveal their answers virtually eliminates the main problems that result from sequential reporting. Consider the question in a tax accounting course on an assignment requiring teams to choose a specific line on a tax form that would pose the greatest financial risk due to an IRS audit. One option would be for the instructor to signal the teams to simultaneously hold up a card with the line number corresponding to their choice (others simultaneous report options are discussed in Sweet, Wright, and Michaelsen, 2008). Requiring a simultaneous public commitment to a specific choice increases both learning and team development because each team is accountable for its choice and motivated to defend its position. Moreover, the more difficult the problem, the greater the potential is for disagreements that are likely to prompt give-and-take discussion, and the teams become more cohesive as they pull together in an attempt to defend their position.

Near the End of the Course. Although TBL provides students with multiple opportunities for learning along the way, instructors can solidify and extend student understanding of both course content and group process issues by reminding students to reflect on what the TBL experience has taught them about course concepts, the value of teams, the kinds of interaction that promote effective teamwork, themselves, and how certain aspects of the course have encouraged positive group norms.

Reinforcing Content Learning. One of the greatest benefits of using TBL is also a potential danger. Since so little class time is aimed at providing students with their initial exposure to course concepts, many fail to realize how much they have learned. In part, this seems to result from the fact that with TBL, the volume of their lecture notes is far less than in typical courses. As a result, some students are a bit uneasy—even if they are aware that the scores from TBL sections on common midterm exams were significantly higher than scores from non-TBL sections. As a result, on an ongoing basis—and especially near the end of the course—instructors should make explicit connections between end-of-course exams and the RAT questions and application assignments. In addition, an effective way to reassure students is devoting a class period to a concept review. In its simplest form, this involves (1) giving students an extensive list of the key concepts from the course, (2) asking them to individually identify any concepts that they do not recognize, (3) compare their conclusions in the teams, and (4) review any concepts that teams identify as needing additional attention.

Learning About the Value of Teams. Concerns about better students being burdened by less motivated or less able peers are commonplace with other group-based instructional approaches. TBL, however, enables instructors to provide students with compelling empirical evidence of the value of teams for tackling difficult intellectual challenges. For example, in taking both individual and team tests, students generally have the impression that the teams are outperforming their own best member, but are seldom aware of either the magnitude or the pervasiveness of the effect. Near the end of each term, we create a transparency that shows cumulative scores from the tests for each team— the low, average, and high member score; the team score; and the difference between the highest member score and the team score (see Michaelsen, Knight, and Fink, 2004). Most students are stunned when they see the pattern of scores for the entire class. In the past twenty years, over 99.9 percent of the nearly sixteen hundred teams in our classes have outperformed their own best member by an average of nearly 11 percent. In fact, in the majority of classes, the lowest team score in the class is higher than the single best individual score in the entire class (Michaelsen, Watson, and Black, 1989).

Recognizing Effective Team Interaction. Over time, teams get increasingly better at ferreting out and using members' intellectual resources in making decisions (Watson, Michaelsen, and Sharp, 1991). However, unless instructors use an activity that prompts members to explicitly think about group process issues, they are likely to miss an important teaching opportunity. This is because most students, although pleased about the results, generally fail to recognize the changes in members' behavior that have made the improvements possible.

We have used two approaches for increasing students' awareness of the relationship between group processes and group effectiveness. The aim of both approaches is to have students reflect on how and why members' interaction patterns have changed as their team became more cohesive. One approach is an assignment that requires students to individually reflect on how the interactions among team members have changed over time and formulate a list of members' actions that made a difference, share their lists with team members, and create a written analysis that summarizes the barriers to their team's effectiveness and what was done to overcome them. The other, and more effective, approach is the same assignment, but students prepare along the way by keeping an ongoing log of observations about how their team has functioned (see Hernandez, 2002).

Learning About Themselves: The Critical Role of Peer Evaluations. One of the most important contributions of TBL is that it creates conditions that can enable students to learn a great deal about the way they interact with others. In large measure, this occurs because of the extensive and intensive interaction within the teams. Over time, members get to know each other's strengths and weaknesses. This makes them better at teaching each other because they can make increasingly accurate assumptions about what a given teammate finds difficult and how best to explain it to that person. In addition, in the vast majority of teams, members develop such strong interpersonal relationships that they feel morally obligated to provide honest feedback to each other to an extent that rarely occurs in other group-based instructional approaches (see Chapter Two, this volume, for examples).

Encouraging the Development of Positive Team Norms. Learning teams will be successful only to the extent that individual members prepare for and attend class. We have learned, however, that when we provide students with ongoing feedback on attendance and individual test scores, the link between preclass preparation and class attendance team performance is so obvious that we can count on norms promoting preclass preparation and attendance pretty much developing on their own. One simple yet effective way to provide such feedback to students is the use of team folders. The folders should contain an ongoing record of each member's attendance, along with the individual and team scores on tests and other assignments (Michaelsen, Knight, and Fink, 2004). The act of recording the scores and attendance data in the team folders is particularly helpful because it ensures that every team member knows how every other team member is doing. Furthermore, promoting public awareness of the team scores fosters norms favoring individual preparation and regular attendance because doing so invariably focuses attention on the fact that there is always a positive relationship between individual preparation and attendance and team performance.

Benefits of Team-Based Learning. In part because of its versatility in dealing with the problems associated with the multiple teaching venues in higher education, TBL produces a wide variety of benefits for students, educational administrators, and individual faculty members who are engaged in the instruction process.

Benefits for Students. In addition to ensuring that students master the basic course content, TBL enables a number of outcomes that are virtually impossible in a lecture-based course format and rarely achieved with any other small group–based instructional approach. When TBL is well implemented, students can progress considerably beyond simply acquiring factual knowledge and achieve a depth of understanding that can come only through solving a series of problems that are too complex for even the best students to complete through their individual effort. In addition, virtually every student develops a deep and abiding appreciation of the value of teams for solving difficult and complex problems. They can gain profound insights into their strengths and weaknesses as learners and as team members.

Compared to a traditional curriculum, faculty members in a wide variety of contexts have observed that introducing TBL enables at-risk students to successfully complete and stay on track in their course work, probably because of the increased social support or peer tutoring.

Benefits from an Administrative Perspective. Many of the benefits for administrators are related to the social impact of the fact that the vast majority of groups develop into effective learning teams. When team-based learning is well implemented:

- Almost without exception, groups develop into effective self-managed learning teams. As a result, faculty and other professional staff time used for training facilitators and involved in team facilitation is minimal.
- TBL is cost-effective since it can be successfully employed in large classes and across academic programs.
- The kinds of assignments characteristic of TBL reduce the potential for interpersonal hostilities within teams to develop to a point where administrators must deal with the personal, political, and possibly even legal aftermath.

Benefits for Faculty. There is tremendous benefit to faculty who use TBL. Because of the student apathy that seems to be an increasingly common response to traditional lecture-based instruction, even the most dedicated faculty tend to burn out. By contrast, TBL prompts most students to engage in the learning process with a level of energy and enthusiasm that transforms classrooms into places of excitement that are rewarding for both them and the instructor. When team-based learning is well implemented:

- Instructors seldom have to worry about students not being in class or failing to prepare for the work that he or she has planned.
- When students are truly prepared for class, interacting with them is much more like working with colleagues than with the empty vessels who tend to show up in lecture–based courses.
- Because instructors spend much more time listening and observing than making formal presentations, they develop many more personally rewarding relationships with their students.

When the instructor adopts the view that the education process is about learning, not about teaching, instructors and students tend to become true partners in the education process.

References

Birmingham, C., and McCord, M. "Group Process Research: Implications for Using Learning Groups." In L. K. Michaelsen, A. B. Knight, and L. D. Fink (eds.), *Team-Based Learning: A Transformative Use of Small Groups in College Teaching.* Sterling, Va.: Stylus, 2004.

Brobeck, F. C., and others. "The Dissemination of Critical, Unshared Information in Decision-Making Groups: The Effects of Pre-Discussion Dissent." *European Journal of Social Psychology,* 2002, *32,* 35–56.

Bruning, R. H., Schraw, G. J., and Ronning, R. R. *Cognitive Psychology and Instruction.* (2nd ed.) Upper Saddle River, N.J.: Prentice Hall, 1994.

Chan, C., Burtis, J., and Bereiter, C. "Knowledge Building as a Mediator of Conflict in Conceptual Change." *Cognition and Instruction,* 1997, *15*(1), 1–40.

Fiechtner, S. B., and Davis, E. A. "Why Some Groups Fail: A Survey of Students' Experiences with Learning Groups." *Organizational Behavior Teaching Review,* 1985, *9*(4), 58–71.

Hattie, J., and Timperley, H. "The Power of Feedback." *Review of Educational Research,* 2007, *77*(1), 81–112.

Hernandez, S. A. "Team-Based Learning in a Marketing Principles Course: Cooperative Structures That Facilitate Active Learning and Higher Level Thinking." *Journal of Marketing Education,* 2002, *24*(1), 45–75.

Johnson, D. W., Johnson, R. T., and Smith, K. "The State of Cooperative Learning in Postsecondary and Professional Settings." *Educational Psychology Review,* 2007, *19*(1), 15–29.

Knight, A. B. "Team-Based Learning: A Strategy for Transforming the Quality of Teaching and Learning." In Michaelsen, L. K., Knight, A. B., and Fink, L. D. (eds.), *Team-Based Learning: A Transformative Use of Small Groups in College Teaching.* Sterling, Va.: Stylus, 2004.

Kulik, J. A., and Kulik, C. C. "Timing of Feedback and Verbal Learning." *Review of Educational Research,* 1988, *58*(1), 79–97.

Lerner, J. S., and Tetlock, P. E. "Accounting for the Effects of Accountability." *Psychological Bulletin,* 1999, *125*(2), 255–275.

Mayer, R. E. "Rote Versus Meaningful Learning." *Theory into Practice,* 2002, *41*(4), 226–232.

McGrath, J. E. "Time, Interaction, and Performance (TIP): A Theory of Groups." *Small Group Research,* 1991, *22*(2), 147–174.

Michaelsen, L. K., and Black, R. H. "Building Learning Teams: The Key to Harnessing the Power of Small Groups in Higher Education." In S. Kadel and J. Keehner (eds.), *Collaborative Learning: A Sourcebook for Higher Education.* State College, Pa.: National Center for Teaching, Learning and Assessment, 1994.

Michaelsen, L. K., Cragin, J. P., and Watson, W. E. "Grading and Anxiety: A Strategy for Coping." *Exchange: The Organizational Behavior Teaching Journal,* 1981, *6*(1), 8–14.

Michaelsen, L. K., Knight, A. B., and Fink, L. D. *Team-Based Learning: A Transformative Use of Small Groups in College Teaching.* Sterling, Va.: Stylus, 2004.

Michaelsen, L. K., and McCord, M. "Teaching Business by Doing Business: An Interdisciplinary Faculty-Friendly Approach." In D. Robertson and L. Nilson (eds.), *To Improve the Academy: Resources for Faculty, Instructional and Organizational Development.* Stillwater, Okla.: New Forums Press, 2006.

Michaelsen, L. K., and Schultheiss, E. E. "Making Feedback Helpful." *Organizational Behavior Teaching Review,* 1988, *13*(1), 109–113.

Michaelsen, L. K., Watson, W. E., and Black, R. H. "A Realistic Test of Individual Versus Group Consensus Decision Making." *Journal of Applied Psychology,* 1989, *74*(5), 834–839.

Miller, J. A. "Experiencing Management: A Comprehensive 'Hands-On' Model for the Introductory Management Course." *Journal of Management Education*, 1991, *15*(2), 151–173.

Millis, B. J., and Cottell, P. G. *Cooperative Learning for Higher Education Faculty*. Phoenix, Ariz.: Oryx Press, 1998.

Pintrich, P. R. "The Role of Metacognitive Knowledge in Learning, Teaching, and Assessing." *Theory into Practice*, 2002, *41*(4), 219–225.

Scandura, J. M. "Instructional Strategies Based on the Structural Learning Theory." In C. M. Reigeluth (ed.), *Instructional Design Theories and Models*. Hillsdale, NJ: Lawrence Erlbaum Associates, 1983.

Sweet, M. "Forming Fair Teams Quickly." In Michaelsen, L., McMahen, K., Levin, R., and Parmalee, D. (eds.) *Team-Based Learning in Health Professions Education*. Sterling, VA: Stylus, 2008.

Sweet, M., Wright, C., and Michaelsen, L. K. "Simultaneous Report: A Reliable Method to Stimulate Class Discussion." *Decision Sciences Journal of Innovative Education*, 2008, *6*(2), 469–473.

Tuckman, B. W. "Developmental Sequences in Small Groups." *Psychological Bulletin*, 1965, *63*, 384–399.

Tuckman, B. W., and Jensen, M.A.C. "Stages in Small Group Development Revisited." *Group and Organizational Studies*, 1977, *2*, 419–427.

Watson, W. E., Kumar, K., and Michaelsen, L. K. "Cultural Diversity's Impact on Group Process and Performance: Comparing Culturally Homogeneous and Culturally Diverse Task Groups." *Academy of Management Journal*, 1993, *36*(3), 590–602.

Watson, W. E., Michaelsen, L. K., and Sharp, W. "Member Competence, Group Interaction and Group Decision-Making: A Longitudinal Study." *Journal of Applied Psychology*, 1991, *76*, 801–809.

Whitehead, A. *The Aims of Education*. Cambridge: Cambridge University Press, 1929.

Wiggins, G., and McTighe, J. H. *Understanding by Design*. Columbus, Ohio: Merrill Prentice Hall, 1998.

Worchel, S., Wood, W., and Simpson, J. A. (eds.). *Group Process and Productivity*. Thousand Oaks, Calif.: Sage, 1992.

LARRY K. MICHAELSEN is professor of management at Central Missouri, David Ross Boyd Professor Emeritus at the University of Oklahoma, a Carnegie Scholar, and former editor of the Journal of Management Education.

MICHAEL SWEET is a faculty development specialist for the Division of Instructional Innovation and Assessment at the University of Texas at Austin.

*Members of a group consider themselves mostly account-
able to an external authority, while members of a team
also hold themselves and each other accountable. In
moments of contribution and accountability, discussions
of course material in the TBL classroom acquire a
remarkable emotional charge.*

The Social Foundation of Team-Based Learning: Students Accountable to Students

Michael Sweet, Laura M. Pelton-Sweet

When I was taking science here at Harvard, it was awfully intim-
idating at times, and . . . it was just *lonely*. You're sort of in your
own world. I didn't know the student's name to my left. I didn't
know the student's name to my right. That's really disconcerting.
        Eric Chehab, Harvard student (Derek Bok Center, 1992)

No man is an island.

                                                                John Donne

The human need for a sense of belonging is deep and powerful and has been
explored by scholars as prominent as Freud (1922), Festinger (1954), and
Schutz (1958), among many others. Following Tinto's book *Leaving College:
Rethinking the Causes and Cures of Student Attrition* (1987), many began
investigating the extent to which a college student's sense of social connec-
tion in the classroom affects variables like academic performance, self-
efficacy, motivation to learn, and perceptions of one's instructor, peers, and
task value (Booker, 2008; Freeman, Anderman, and Jensen, 2007; Pittman
and Richmond, 2007; Summers, Beretvas, Svinicki, and Gorin, 2005).
    Given this growing understanding of the social dimension of the class-
room, it is no surprise that positive emotional and motivational effects of

WILEY
InterScience®
DISCOVER SOMETHING GREAT

NEW DIRECTIONS FOR TEACHING AND LEARNING, no. 116, Winter 2008 © Wiley Periodicals, Inc.
Published online in Wiley InterScience (www.interscience.wiley.com) • DOI: 10.1002/tl.331

various forms of small group learning have become fairly well documented (Johnson and Johnson, 1989; Johnson, Johnson, and Smith, 2007; Boekarts and Minnaert, 2006; Natasi and Clements, 1991). As one form of small group learning, team-based learning's unique sequence of individual and group work with immediate feedback enables and encourages students to engage course content and each other in remarkable ways. Specifically, team-based learning (TBL) creates an environment where students can fulfill their human need to belong in the process of negotiating and mastering course content with their teammates.

What sets TBL apart from other forms of small group learning is its accountability structure—a rhythm of moments in which students' social and intellectual experiences of the classroom become interlocked and amplified. The first chapter in this volume describes the system of incentives and communication channels that a TBL instructor sets up to enable these moments. This chapter shows what these moments look like and how students' social interaction in those moments cultivates their abilities to learn from and with one another.

Accountability: The Conceptual Bridge Between the Student and the Team

If the need to belong can be considered a motivational fuel, then accountability is the engine that transforms that fuel into instructional mileage. Of course, grades are the instrumental mechanisms that ensure accountability in TBL, but those who have never been in a classroom with students getting immediate feedback during a team readiness assessment test (tRAT) have not seen the expressive mechanisms with which students position themselves and each other moment to moment in terms of accountability for their understanding of the course content. This process is important because it reveals the extent to which the social experience of team membership can motivate students into deeper engagement with the course material. A sense of belonging is based on having close and positive relationships to members of a group: if the goal of a group is to perform well academically, then members who clearly and repeatedly prevent the group from doing well will likely find relationships with their teammates becoming less close and less positive. This is the negative consequence students risk when they attempt to persuade their team to accept one answer or another. Such attempts position them—for better or worse—as accountable at some level for the group's outcome.

In a review, Lerner and Tetlock (1999) described accountability as a useful bridge between the individual and group levels of analysis. They defined accountability as the "expectation that one may be called on to justify one's beliefs, feelings, and actions to others" (p. 255), emphasizing that accountability usually implies positive or negative consequences arising from how one's justifications are evaluated by those others. Common sense dictates that the more one actually cares about the evaluation of those others, the more important one's accountability to them becomes. As we will see, students express this caring in the form of tremendous anxiety around the possibility of "leading their team astray" or "getting it wrong for the team" and being "mad at themselves" when they do.

Because of its emphasis on critical thinking, Lerner and Tetlock's synthesis of the literature seems particularly relevant to teachers:

> Self-critical and effortful thinking is most likely to be activated when decision makers learn prior to forming any opinions that they will be accountable to an audience (a) whose views are unknown, (b) who is interested in accuracy, (c) who is interested in processes rather than specific outcomes, (d) who is reasonably well informed, and (e) who has a legitimate reason for inquiring into the reasons behind participants' judgments [1999, p. 259].

This synthesis is good news for TBL practitioners because for the most part, it describes the conditions that TBL students face when they come together for the tRAT. Having just finished their individual tests, the students do not yet know how their teammates answered each question, but they can expect their teammates to be interested in accuracy, to be reasonably well informed, and to have a legitimate reason for wanting to talk about the test. Whether a student's teammates are more interested in process than outcome is mostly out of the teacher's hands, as it will likely vary with the individual achievement goal orientations (learning versus performance) of each teammate (Dweck, 1999).

In the following sections, we listen in on actual conversations among TBL students, focusing on how accountability is made salient among team members from moment to moment. Our goal is first to identify in transcript excerpts how that accountability indexing occurs and the social pressures associated with it. We then consider excerpts showing how that social atmosphere stimulates teams to use every intellectual resource its members possess. All quotations come directly from recordings of TBL students in college classrooms taking tRATs.

Accountability Anxiety: Awareness of Teammate Judgments. As a result of the buildup to a team decision and immediate feedback, the apprehensiveness about the possibility of getting it wrong for the team can be intense. Consider the following excerpt in which a team debates the answer to a multiple-choice question about the characteristics of long-term memory:

STUDENT 5: I'm leaning towards E, but I don't want to be the one to miss it—
[laughter]
STUDENT 2: Yeah, I thought it was E too, but I am not sure.

STUDENT 5: 'Cause, yeah, I was looking over it before I turned it in, and I changed it from B to E, like right before I handed it in, so . . .

STUDENT 6: Yeah

STUDENT 4: Cause E could totally be . . . yeah, goal setting. . . . whatever.

STUDENT 5: Um, what do you say on 15?

STUDENT 6: I said E. But I mean, it's just like—

STUDENT 3: I said B.

STUDENT 6: [reads aloud] "distinguishing between important and unimportant information."

STUDENT 2: I said E, because to me it seemed like you weren't focusing on main ideas . . .

STUDENT 4: I'll go with E, I don't care.

STUDENT 5: Maybe they'll remember that more than something else. . . . Let's just—

STUDENT 6:   Right. Like it's in their memory longer.

STUDENT 5: I say E. I'm scared. But that's what I say.

STUDENT 6: [laughs] It's all built up now, like "Oh god! What are we gonna do?!"

[laughter]

STUDENT 4: We'll go with E. [Scratching. . .] . . . correct. Yay.

STUDENT 5: And it's right

STUDENT 2: Yay!

STUDENT 6: Fantastic. That's awesome. We rock.

Here student 5 expresses intense emotion around the possibility of being accountable as "the one to miss it" for the team, even saying she is "scared." In other excerpts, this anxiety manifests in phrases like, "Please don't be mad if it's wrong," "Don't get mad," and "I'm nervous" in the lead-up to a scratch on an IF-AT card (see Chapter One for a discussion of IF-ATs). Student 6 even observes the emotional tension and jokes about it being "all built up, like, 'Oh god! What are we gonna do!'" Finally, they scratch the covering off the box on the answer sheet, and answer E turns out to be correct. Relieved celebration—"Yay!" and "We rock"—frequently follows a tense debate leading to the team's getting the right answer, taking many forms like, "Thank God," "Yessssss," "Genius," and "Good job, y'all."

After a tense debate leading to the team's choosing the wrong answer, emotional words and frustrated confusion—"What?! How can that *not* be B?!"—sometimes follow. As we will see below, the experience of having "led the team astray" can be emotionally upsetting for many students, and the memory of it "haunts" them, guiding their future behavior.

Putting It on the Line: Accepting Accountability for One's Answer. Before the answer is revealed, students sometimes make flat statements of certainty: "I was sure about that one," or "I am pretty positive it's

A," or even, "It's probably E; I'm probably right." Alternatively, they can hesitantly accept accountability in the form of preemptive apologies:

STUDENT 4: I am sure you're right, but . . .
STUDENT 1: I hope. If I put it wrong, I am sorry.
STUDENT 4: No problem.
STUDENT 3: [scratching to reveal the answer] Yep, it's A. Cool.

In an example of a fairly common occurrence, a student decides that he or she has been convinced enough by another student to agree, though the qualifying "but . . ." tagged on at the end of a student's agreement indicates reservations. This lukewarm agreement manifests in several ways, often with some form of mitigating pseudo-conditional ("I could go with D" or "I would be willing to go with C"). Here student 1 seems to sense student 4's discomfort and follows up by acknowledging that she "hopes" her answer is right and preemptively apologizing if it is not, thereby accepting accountability herself for the outcome. The preemptive apology ("I apologize in advance if I was wrong") is a common form of a student's acknowledging accountability, for better or worse. Here, however, student 1 is reassured that nothing will be held against her, and student 3 reveals that student 1's answer was in fact correct.

After an answer is revealed, positive accountability claims are somewhat rare, but include "I was right" and "Genius" (referring to oneself). Negative accountability claims are more common and are almost always apologies—": "Sorry" and "sorry, y'all" and even "Shit—sorry!" Forgiveness for negative accountability admission sometimes follows, such as, "It's all good" and "It happens" and "Don't worry about it." Overt statements of blame are actually made by students very rarely.

Clearly the language and intensity of these excerpts argue for the fact that something emotional is at stake in these moments when a group is deciding to go with one member's answer and in the celebration or fallout after the answer is revealed. For teachers, overhearing the extent to which students can become impassioned in their discussions about their course content is always delightful and can sometimes be overwhelming!

"Don't Look at Me": Attempts to Avoid Accountability. Because moments of accountability are when students risk losing face and possibly even marginalization by their group, it is probably not surprising that efforts to avoid accountability are nearly ubiquitous. Three forms of this behavior are abstaining, hedging, and conforming.

Abstaining comments mostly involve flatly refusing to even suggest an answer—"No comment," "I completely guessed," "I'm not even going to argue for mine," and "I have nothing to say about that one." Infrequently, students abstain from whole blocks of questions: "Okay, I've got question marks by 11 to 13, so don't trust me on any of those!"

Hedging comments include a suggested answer and a qualification of some kind—": "I'm leaning toward C" and "I said B, but I guessed." Hedges are actually so common that statements without a hedge stand out as exceptions in the transcripts.

Conforming occurs in two ways, both of which involve students' expressing their refusal to go it alone in the face of disagreement. In pursuit of consensus, students occasionally defer to the majority: "It's really whatever y'all want to put," "We can just go with the majority," and "Since y'all both put it, I'll go with that one." Alternatively, a student on the cusp of having the group choose the answer he or she advocated may refuse sole accountability, in effect voting against the answer if he or she is the only one willing to argue for it. This appears in statements such as: "Someone else has to vote for it, because if I'm wrong, I don't want to be the only one that's wrong—I don't want to lead the whole team astray" and "If it was just me, I would still say B, but I don't want to say that and be wrong." The following sequence is an example of refusing sole accountability, with an interesting follow-up comment from another team member:

STUDENT 2:   I don't want to be the only one thinking it's irrelevant and then get it wrong, so . . . .
STUDENT 4:   Well, last time I pushed for something, and I got it wrong twice.

Here, student 2 verbalizes his worries about being accountable for a wrong answer. Student 4 then commiserates, sharing his memory of having "pushed for something" and gotten it wrong twice. Importantly, the *tone* of student 4's voice gives his comment a sense of gentle warning, as if an unstated "so think hard about this" actually concludes what he is trying to communicate.

Although excerpts like these are provocative, they do not tell us how frequently this emotionally laden performance tracking occurs. Therefore, we conducted a survey across two classes, asking them about their experience of convincing their team of a wrong answer or being convinced of a wrong answer (leading others astray or being led astray). They reported changing their behavior as a result of leading others astray overwhelmingly more often than they reported holding it against others who had led them astray. In other words, students were far more forgiving of others' mistakes than their own.

From fifty-three returned surveys, thirty-one said that they had convinced their team of a wrong answer. Of that thirty-on students, nineteen (or 61 percent) said that the experience influenced their later behavior, describing the effect in the following ways:

"I prepared more."
"I wasn't as confident with my next answer."
"I didn't want to tell them another wrong answer."
"I was more cautious and got support."

"It made me a little apprehensive."

"I was more careful to ask for feedback from my group."

"I was more cautious." (submitted twice)

"I was more cautious about my future answers."

"It made me want to look at both solutions thoroughly next time I did a problem."

"Be more careful to do team activity."

"Was more careful in the future when reading."

"It made me more resolved about saying what I am 'sure' of."

"I made sure I really knew the material before I confidently convinced them of my answer."

"Just more careful about being too assertive."

"Mad at myself because I let my team down."

"I felt bad I got a question wrong for my team."

"I made sure to speak up when I absolutely knew the answer."

"I learned to listen to others more and not just go with my gut instinct."

However, forty-six said a team member had convinced *them* of a wrong answer, but of that forty-six only seven (15 percent) said the experience influenced their later behavior. They described the effect as follows:

"It made me want them to show me how they arrived at the answer."

"We were more skeptical of that person."

"I did not trust them as much."

"I always have to think twice when they say an answer."

"I was more cautious and asked them to explain how they got that answer."

"I may be slightly more skeptical in the future."

"I was less willing to listen if it happened consistently."

So far, both transcript and survey evidence suggest that TBL's accountability structure creates moments where a student's public contribution to the team can have lasting socioemotional effects for everyone on their team. This history of accountability motivates students to become familiar with and continually revise their estimates of each other's expertise to make sure the team brings the best of its collective strengths to bear on any given question. It is this familiarity that enables students to coregulate each other's learning in the group setting.

Coregulated learning is a relatively new construct in educational psychology and extends self-regulated learning research into regulation that takes place between learners. In TBL, coregulated learning can occur based on teammates' familiarity with each other's general performance ("He's usually right, dude! I mean, your choice is pretty good"), specific study skills like good note taking ("She has like this exact sentence in her notes"), or, as in the following excerpt, careful reading habits:

STUDENT 6: Well, I'd go with A. I put D but—

STUDENT 1: I put D too, but . . .

STUDENT 2: I put D.

STUDENT 3: I put D, but . . .

STUDENT 4: Well!

[group laughter]

STUDENT 4: Well, then someone argue for D and then someone argue for A, and we'll figure it out.

STUDENT 6: I don't even have a good argument.

STUDENT 1: It just seems more logical to me, that's all. D sort of seems more logical, but . . .

STUDENT 4: Yeah, I just, I remember reading A and not D. That's the only thing why I would not change it.

STUDENT 1: Yeah, if you remember reading it. I would be willing to trust your reading it more than my logic.

STUDENT 6: Yeah, we're just trying to justify it. I don't remember reading anything on contextual views, so. . . .

STUDENT 4: Yeah, I don't remember contextual views. . . . Maybe, well I think "contextual," that means like what it has to do with . . . that's why I put A because if you learn something . . . I don't know . . .

STUDENT 6: And then be able to apply it . . .

STUDENT 5: In other contexts . . .

STUDENT 4: Yeah.

STUDENT 1: Maybe A is the best answer

STUDENT 6: Yeah. [sigh] I think we should just do it.

STUDENT 4: But I'd hate to say it and it be wrong.

STUDENT 1: I know [laughing]

The coregulation here is interesting for at least two reasons. First, most of the team members had chosen answer D, but student 4's reputation for being a careful reader and her choice of A persuaded the team of the correct answer. In this case, a simple vote would have failed the team. But knowing student 4 as well as they did enabled them to consider her opinion with an appropriate amount of weight. Second, the team verbalized their intellectual attempts to justify answer A. This process of evaluating and explaining the contents of one's thoughts in real time is called *type 3 concurrent verbalization,* and there is a strong research base for its value as a metacognitive strategy in problem-solving activities (Hacker and Dunlosky, 2003). In TBL, this kind of collaborative, coregulated learning discussion becomes increasingly common as the course unfolds. This unfolding process was documented empirically by Watson, Michaelsen, and Sharp (1991), who found that although team scores increased at every measure, teams became less reliant on their highest-performing member over time. For teachers, this process is thrilling.

Practical Lessons We Learned from Our Teams. The following suggestions come from years of experience, as well as the fortunate circumstance of having both transcript and performance data for the same teams:

- *When organizing students into teams, consider including anxiety about the course topic among the student characteristics to be distributed across teams.* One of TBL's virtues is that it draws on students' socioemotional needs to propel them deeper into the course content. Team membership seems to meet students' need to belong at some level, but as our transcripts show, moments of accountability put that belonging at risk and can be nerve-racking. The famous Yerkes-Dodson curve illustrates the point that while some anxiety can focus attention and improve learning, too much anxiety can overwhelm the learner and inhibit performance (for a discussion, see Svinicki, 2004). It seems to us that piling content-related anxiety on top of accountability anxiety for many members of the same team should be avoided. For many, some classes come preloaded with an emotional charge (examples are mathematics for nonmajors, human sexuality, difficult gateway classes), and we recommend that teachers of these classes discretely collect information about students' experience of that emotional charge at the beginning of the term and include it in the team formation process. This data collection is easily accomplished using a "get to know you" questionnaire, which many teachers already use.
- *Enable and encourage vote splitting.* Michaelsen, Knight, and Fink (2004) described their method of using a split-answer format on individual RATs: they allow students to answer each question three times, with each of those answers being worth one point. In this way, students can indicate their level of confidence in an answer and leave room for negotiation by splitting their vote. Interestingly, our transcripts document that students discovered the value of this practice even when tests are not formatted in this way.

In transcripts of two groups in the same class, one team got better at working together over time and one team got worse as measured by the synergy ratios of each team (for a description of synergy ratio calculation, see Watson, Michaelsen, and Sharp, 1991). Without any external encouragement to do so in this case, both teams developed a linguistic practice of splitting their vote from the outset, which appeared as reporting which two possible answers a student was "between," "torn between," "stuck between," "hung up on," or "couldn't decide between." In terms of accountability, this strategy gives individuals flexibility to discuss a range of options instead of forcing them immediately into anxiety-laden all-or-nothing accountability positions. Across the semester, members of the team that got better at working together over time split their votes nearly four times as often as the team that got worse. Although this is only a single example from one class, these transcript data add weight to the argument by Michaelsen, Knight, and Fink that the split-choice kind of RAT helps students and teams.

Teachers can encourage a similar vote-splitting effect at the team level by allowing teams to receive partial credit for second and third attempts to answer a RAT question correctly, as described in Chapter One.

- *Encourage teams to table and return to questions when discussion stalls.* The emotional buildup to the revelation of an answer (which one student called "the moment of truth") can be tense, and sometimes teams are not confident enough in any one answer to push them over that threshold. In these moments, a member occasionally suggests the team skip that question or asks, "Should we come back to this one?" We all recognize this as a good test-taking strategy for individuals, and in terms of accountability, this enables students to gather more information about who among their teammates has better mastery of the course material from the feedback on subsequent test questions, so they can return to the tabled question with a different set of self and coregulatory perspectives. In our research, members of the team who learned to work better over time tabled and returned to almost five times as many questions as the team that got worse at working together.

- *Conduct formative peer assessment at least once prior to summative assessment at the end of the term.* Peer assessments are covered in depth in Chapter Five in this volume. However, because this chapter is about how TBL can tap into students' need to belong and the instructional effects of accountability, we would be remiss not to mention the role that peer assessment can and should play in this process. We believe peer assessments that require students to write something to or about their teammates (instead of or in addition to assigning numerical points) can be an important stimulus to both individual learning and a sense of belonging. We require students to write at least one thing they appreciate about and one thing they request from each of their teammates. Although pointed requests are made a respectable number of the times (for example, "Please come prepared" and "Listen to others more"), these messages between students are overwhelmingly positive and even encouraging (for example, "Speak up more; you're usually right when you do" and "Keep up the good work"). Opening this textual channel between students enables them to exchange messages that nourish the sense of being seen, heard, and valued by teammates.

- *Be prepared for the students to hold you accountable in new ways.* When it comes time for instructor feedback following a readiness assurance process, keep in mind that students have gone through a great deal. They have (1) thought through the test questions on their own and made intellectual commitments to certain answers, (2) considered many angles of the questions in subsequent discussion with their team, (3) gone through the potentially nerve-racking experience of public accountability for answers they felt strongly about, and (4) experienced whatever emotional consequences that accountability brings. As a result of this intense, socially charged, and content-focused experience, teams can become attached to their answer choices and vigorous in their desire for their instructor to explain and even defend why he or she keyed the correct answer as he or she did. While many college classrooms have a handful of passionate students, do not underestimate the emotional power of what we jokingly refer to as the "unionized" passion in the TBL classroom. While it may seem strange to warn teachers that they may have to face a room of passionately motivated students, not every teacher is ready to flexibly facilitate the energies at play in the fully activated TBL classroom. For advice on what success in this situation requires, see Chapter Four, this volume.

References

Birmingham, C., and Michaelsen, L. K. "Conflict Resolution in Decision Making Teams: A Longitudinal Study." Paper presented at the Midwest Academy of Management, Chicago, 1999.

Boekarts, M., and Minnaert, A. "Affective and Motivational Outcomes of Working in Collaborative Groups." *Educational Psychology*, 2006, 26(2), 187–208.

Booker, K. "The Role of Instructors and Peers in Establishing Classroom Community." *Journal of Instructional Psychology*, 2008, 35(1), 12–16.

Derek Bok Center for Teaching and Learning. *Thinking Together: Collaborative Learning in Science*. Cambridge, Mass.: Harvard University, 1992.

Dweck, C. S. *Self-Theories: Their Role in Motivation, Personality, and Development*. Ann Arbor, Mich.: Edwards Brothers, 1999.

Festinger, L. "A Theory of Social Comparison Processes." *Human Relationships*, 1954, 7, 117–140.

Freeman, T. M., Anderman, L. H., and Jensen, J. M. "Sense of Belonging in College Freshmen at the Classroom and Campus Levels." *Journal of Experimental Education*, 2007, 75(3), 203–220.

Freud, S. *Group Psychology and the Analysis of the Ego* (J. Strachey, trans.). London: International Psycho-Analytical Press, 1922.

Hacker, D. J., and Dunlosky, J. "Not All Metacognition Is Created Equal." *Problem-Based Learning in the Information Age*. New Directions for Teaching and Learning, no. 95. San Francisco: Jossey-Bass, 2003.

Johnson, D. W., and Johnson, R. T. *Cooperation and Competition Theory and Research*. Edina, Minn.: Interaction Book Co., 1989.

Johnson, D. W., Johnson, R. T., and Smith, K. "The State of Cooperative Learning in Postsecondary and Professional Settings." *Educational Psychology Review*, 2007, 19(1), 15–29.

Lerner, J. S., and Tetlock, P. E. "Accounting for the Effects of Accountability." *Psychological Bulletin*, 1999, 125(2), 255–275.

Michaelsen, L. K., Knight, A. B., and Fink, L. D. (eds.). *Team-Based Learning: A Transformative Use of Small Groups in College Teaching*. Sterling, Va.: Stylus, 2004.

Natasi, B. K., and Clements D. H. "Research on Cooperative Learning: Implications for Practice." *School Psychology Review*, 1991, 20(1), 110–131.

Pittman, L. D., and Adeya, R. "Academic and Psychological Functioning in Late Adolescence: The Importance of School and Belonging." *Journal of Experimental Education*, 2007, 75(4), 270–290.

Pittman, L. D., and Richmond, A. "University Belonging, Friendship Quality, and Psychological Adjustment during the Transition to College." *The Journal of Experimental Education*, 2007, 76(4), 343–362.

Schutz, W. *FIRO: A Three-Dimensional Theory of Interpersonal Behavior*. New York: Holt, 1958.

Summers, J. J., Beretvas, S. N., Svinicki, M. D., and Gorin, J. S. "Evaluating Collaborative Learning and Community." *Journal of Experimental Education*, 2005, 73(3), 165–188.

Svinicki, M. D. *Learning and Motivation in the Postsecondary Classroom*. Bolton, Mass.: Anker, 2004.

Tinto, V. *Leaving College: Rethinking the Causes and Cures of Student Attrition*. Chicago: University of Chicago Press, 1987.

Watson, W. E., Michaelsen, L. K., and Sharp, W. "Member Competence, Group Interaction and Group Decision-Making: A Longitudinal Study." *Journal of Applied Psychology*, 1991, 76(6), 801–80

MICHAEL SWEET is a faculty development specialist for the Division of Instructional Innovation and Assessment at the University of Texas at Austin.

LAURA M. PELTON-SWEET is a counselor at Phoenix Academy in Austin, Texas.

NEW DIRECTIONS FOR TEACHING AND LEARNING • DOI: 10.1002/tl

Professional schools must cultivate specific competencies within their students in order to prepare them for their professions, and these competencies are changing. Team-based learning is ideally suited to meet the demands placed on professional schools as they confront new challenges.

Knowledge Is No Longer Enough: Enhancing Professional Education with Team-Based Learning

Jim Sibley, Dean X. Parmelee

The explosion of information and increasing complexity of the modern workplace have placed new burdens and demands on professional schools and programs. Professional schools, such as those in business, engineering, and the health professions, have come under increasing scrutiny as the required exit competencies for graduates have shifted from knowing information to being able to solve complex problems, communicate clearly, collaborate effectively, and use lifelong learning skills. It has become clear that professional schools must make changes in both curricula and pedagogy.

This chapter first describes increased competency-based demands in professional schools and how small group learning is well suited to cultivate those competencies. It then singles out team-based learning (TBL) as a particularly powerful form of small group learning by distinguishing it from other forms of small group learning, charting its recent growth in professional schools and offering some tips for professional school faculty interested in implementing TBL. Finally, it turns to professional school students themselves by reporting—in their own words—how they have experienced various features of TBL—powerful testimony as to how TBL can and does meet the competency-based challenges that professional schools face today.

NEW DIRECTIONS FOR TEACHING AND LEARNING, no. 116, Winter 2008 © Wiley Periodicals, Inc.
Published online in Wiley InterScience (www.interscience.wiley.com) • DOI: 10.1002/tl.332

Cultivating Competencies: What Small Group Learning Brings to Professional Education

Professional schools define what their graduates should be able to do in the professional workplace by the time they graduate. Accrediting bodies have designated these expected outcomes as *competencies,* and the term *competency* is defined by Govaerts (2008) as "an individual's ability to make deliberate choices from a repertoire of behaviors for handling situations and tasks in specific contexts of professional practice." He reminds us that "competencies are context-dependent and always imply integration of knowledge, skills, judgment and attitudes" (p. 42).

The traditional didactic, instructor-centric model has been the focus of much negative attention in educational community in recent years. The image of the content expert filling up empty vessels is still strongly held by many faculty and students. A lucid and engaging presentation can be well received by students and pleasurable to give, but it may not do much to develop the new required exit competencies. There are compelling studies on the poor efficacy of lectures and the limited short-term and long-term impacts on learning (Bligh, 2000; Freire, 2000; McKeachie, 1986). Clearly new approaches are required to design programs and educational experiences that will develop the knowledge, skills, and judgment students need for their professional careers.

Professional school faculty are transforming knowledge-focused curricula to ones in which the goals and objectives of units of study go beyond simple mastery of the content, for example, "know Ohm's Law," "understand Krebs cycle," or "describe an ideal marketing plan." Traditionally instructors have listed all the important content topic areas, assigned them to the time slot allotted for the course, designated who teaches what, then used a final exam to determine whether the learners have acquired the knowledge. This traditional approach, however, does not promote the development of professional competencies.

Clarity has been growing that instructional design at the professional school level must emphasize the mastery of content in order to apply it— a much greater challenge than "covering content." This transformation requires a new approach to the design of courses and to teaching and learning. The overarching goal becomes significant learning (Fink, 2003)— learning that endures well beyond the end of the course. It also increases the responsibility of the faculty, who now must design and orchestrate learning activities and assessments that enable students first to master the knowledge and then apply it to increasingly complex problems.

As professional schools have evolved toward competency-based education, active learner-centered strategies have become increasingly important. The professions have expressed a need for students who can communicate, value teamwork, solve problems, acquire knowledge that is broad and deep, and do so for their entire career.

NEW DIRECTIONS FOR TEACHING AND LEARNING • DOI: 10.1002/tl

Communication Skills. Communication skills are of the cornerstones of professional practice. How one says something is often perceived as being as important as what is said.

The development of communication skills is first encouraged during team test discussions in TBL and then by the appeals process that allows teams to generate a scholarly written argument to appeal their grade on any question in readiness assurance tests. Next, the students engage in lower-stakes intrateam activity reporting discussions and then progress to the higher-stakes interteam activity reporting discussion. Students get to practice their discourse within their team before they publicly commit to a position and then must publicly defend their decisions while questioning the decisions and decision-making processes of those around them. These kinds of discussions can promote higher-level reasoning, deeper-level understanding, and long-term retention (Johnson and Johnson, 2004).

When we create activities that lead to intellectual conflict and then facilitate discussion constructively, we help students reach a higher-level of reasoning, encourage divergent thinking, foster creativity, and promote long-term retention (Johnson and Johnson, 1995).

Valuing Teams. Many students and instructors have had poor team experiences, so it is very important to instill in students the value and power of working in teams. This can be difficult in academic cultures that routinely celebrate individual achievement and success. Many positive aspects of teaming can be demonstrated to students with TBL.

As teams become more cohesive and more effective, they can begin to recognize the hallmarks of good team behaviors: improvements in communication skills; a willingness to divide effort fairly; generosity in giving credit; the ability to constructively provide criticism as well as to care, share, and support others; and the embracing of team spirit. Students begin to recognize that "teams can give individuals insights and understandings that could never be achieved alone" (Johnson and Johnson, 2004, p. 9).

Problem Solving and Critical Thinking. The crafting of good problems is one of the keys to success in team-based learning. Problems can be crafted to increase in difficulty as the students' problem-solving skills progress. Serial problems with slight shifts in context can help students develop problem-solving skills that are not context bound. The discourse within the teams and during reporting activities allows students to explore other students' thinking and articulate their own thinking more clearly.

Many factors are important in the development of expert problem-solving skills. TBL creates opportunities for students to develop these skills aided by the frequent feedback from their teammates and the instructor. It is helpful to remember that problem solving often occurs in team settings, where "individuals share in problem solving and contribute to group success, in which problems are not well defined and decision makers have imperfect knowledge and in which no single best answer is readily available" (Hunt, Haidet, Coverdale, and Richards, 2003, p. 13).

The recognition of gaps in one's knowledge (metacognition) and development of task-focused energy to seek relevant information is the first key to expert problem solving. Metacognition has been described by Bransford as "an internal conversation" (2000, p. 21). Team-based learning provides many opportunities for students to engage with this conversation, which is externalized in both intrateam and interteam discussions. This can be key to the identification of knowledge gaps for students. These gaps revealed during team discussions, simultaneous reporting, and the full class reporting discussions can be a powerful motivator for continued learning.

Another struggle for students, especially in the health professions, is to remain problem minded for as long as possible and avoid the rush to solution or diagnosis. Adequately examining, defining, and establishing the nature of the problem is key to finding good solutions. TBL provides many opportunities to defend one's thinking and examine others' problem-solving processes. Another factor important to problem solving is the recognition that context can have large effects on the desirability of a solution. In TBL we have the ability to present a series of activities based on the similar problems, which allows students the chance to examine the effect of detail and context on a reasonable solution.

Depth versus Breadth. The depth-versus-breadth debate is a source of tension in most curriculum redevelopment projects. At first glance, it seems intuitively obvious that sacrificing breadth of coverage for depth of learning may leave students with gaps in their knowledge. However, the question that must be asked is whether it is possible to cover everything the student will need in professional practice in the undergraduate curriculum. Hung (2004, p. 14) and others believe that this is not possible or even desirable since "knowledge is constantly expanding, and we question the possibility that any course, or program of studies, can provide a full understanding of a content's breadth" (p. 14). If it is not possible to cover the breadth of a subject area, should we not then help students acquire the lifelong learning and problem-solving skills that will allow them to research and solve new problems as they arise in their professional practice? Many curricular experts now believe that superficial coverage must be replaced with "learning with understanding" (Bransford, 2000, p. 8).

In a study that compared outcomes from didactic lecturing to an active learning strategy in a large group setting, Haidet and others (2004) found that "the teacher was able to cover the same amount of conceptually complex and mathematically-oriented content in the active session as in the didactic session with no detrimental effects on short- or long-term knowledge acquisition or attitude enhancement" (p. 23). Another study that compared examination performance in a second-year pathology curriculum found no significant difference in student performance when comparing a case-based group discussion cohort to a team-based learning cohort (Koles and others, 2005). This is consistent with findings from the University of

British Columbia Engineering school (T. Froese, personal communication, April 2005). Koles, Stolfi, and Parmelee (2008) compared the examination performance of students in a second-year medical school class on questions related to material taught only in TBL format versus standard lecture format. There was significantly better performance for the class as a whole on questions related to material covered in the TBL portion, and the effect was even stronger in students in the lower quartile of the class.

Lifelong Learning. With the ever-expanding world of information, we must foster lifelong learning skills in students. Gone are the days of professional schools' providing a lifetime of knowledge. The ability to critically read and process information from a variety of sources is key to a successful professional life. Ryan (2008) has highlighted many positive learning outcomes resulting from required preclass readings. They can help students become familiar with the nature of the literature in their discipline and help them to process and retrieve relevant information quickly. Ryan writes, "Most students don't preview and scan the text before reading, as expert readers usually do. We help students understand and appreciate how professional and technical material is formally presented. . . . This will better prepare them for what they will be asked to do later in most professions" (n.p.) When students are required to read the preparatory material, discussions in class will likely be more thoughtful and more engaging, not just for the instructor but for the students as well. A student who comes to class prepared and with background knowledge is transformed from a passive to an active learner.

Team-Based Learning: A Powerful Form of Small Group Learning

Team-based learning is a powerful form of small group learning. In this section, we first distinguish TBL from problem-based learning, chart TBL's growth in professional school settings in recent years, and offer some advice to professional school faculty interested in implementing TBL.

Team-Based Learning Versus Problem-Based Learning. Given the professional competencies necessary now and how TBL supports their instruction, it is appropriate to acknowledge that some instructors have been using problem-based learning (PBL) to achieve the same affect. Indeed, PBL has been heralded by some as the answer to creating the professionals of tomorrow. In problem-based learning, students are presented a problem to solve and must determine for themselves what information is important within the problem and what information is still needed before a solution can be proposed. Students in PBL often work collaboratively, with small groups guided by "tutors," who ensure that conversation stays productive.

PBL and TBL share some of the same pedagogical virtues, but PBL places significantly greater resource demands on the institution than does TBL. For example, PBL faculty-to-student ratios have been reported in the range of six to one (Hunt, Haidet, Coverdale, and Richards, 2003) and eight to one (A. Bradley, personal communication, April 2007). The University of British Columbia Medical School has over four hundred PBL tutors and uses seventy tutors in any particular week (Amanda Bradley, personal communication, April 2007). This requirement for large amounts of faculty time, administrative support, and physical space can make PBL unsuitable for many schools.

In contrast, TBL is well suited to achieve similar good student outcomes while conserving precious resources, since it is scalable to much larger student-to-faculty ratios of two hundred to one and above (Hunt, Haidet, Coverdale, and Richards, 2003) and can be facilitated in large classroom settings.

From our experience and that of others, we have become convinced that TBL provides an enormous opportunity for faculty to become more fully engaged with their students than with lecture-based instruction or other small group format such as PBL.

The Growth of Team-Based Learning in Professional Education. In 2001, the U.S. Department of Education awarded a grant to explore the use of team-based learning in medical education to Baylor Medical College. This award funded several years of nationwide workshops for faculty, direct support to medical schools to implement the strategy, and further support for its dissemination. Several medical schools were searching for ways to have more active learning instead of a steady stream of lectures. However, they chose not to develop a PBL curriculum because of its high student-to-faculty ratio requirements. Instead, several of these schools sent key faculty to workshops on TBL.

Many returned to their home campuses and either converted entire courses to the TBL strategy (Nieder, Parmelee, Stolfi, and Hudes, 2005) or began to use it episodically in place of existing faculty-led small group discussions. Within several years, several publications indicated the positive academic and noncognitive outcomes of TBL in medical education (Dunaway, 2005; Kelly and others, 2005; Koles and others, 2005; Vasan and DeFouw, 2005; Searle and others, 2003; Baldwin, Bedell, and Johnson, 1997). Schools of nursing, veterinary medicine, dentistry, physicians' assistants, and other allied health professions programs have also developed TBL within existing curricular structures.

The popularity of TBL in engineering education has increased. Engineering programs have long been synonymous with teamwork, but the TBL methodology had been used in only a small number of engineering courses in various institutions, such as the University of Oklahoma, University of Kentucky (L. Michaelsen, personal communication, June 2008), and the University of Missouri-Rolla (Weeks, 2003) prior to 2004. TBL in engineering schools began to see more widespread implementations in 2004–2005, with the University of British Columbia's (UBC) second-year mechanical design course (Ostafichuk and Hodgson, 2005) and a fourth-year construction management course (Froese, 2005). At the same time, the University of Kentucky, with the help of Derek Lane, was redeveloping its civil engineering capstone project course to incorporate TBL (Yost and Lane, 2007). Since these first courses, a large number of courses at UBC have been delivered successfully using the TBL format. These courses have ranged from the softer skills courses like Technology and Society to "hard" skill courses in the engineering sciences like Aerodynamics and Orthopedic Biomechanics.

Implementing TBL in Professional School Settings. A number of elements are critical for successful implementation of TBL in a professional school setting:

- The institutional culture, including the students, must support instructional innovation and understand that a new strategy has a trial-and-error period. The faculty member initiating TBL must be open to and welcome ongoing feedback from the students, seeking their thoughts on how to make a module stronger.
- The instructor must prepare well ahead. Unlike lecture preparation, which can sometimes be done at the last minute because one has done it so many times, writing a good TBL module takes an enormous effort, and peer review is very helpful before trying it out with students. Fortunately, once a module has been delivered and adjusted for the inevitable glitches, it can be used again and again with little additional preparation.
- The instructor will have to embrace the philosophy of developing learner-centered activities for classroom time and become comfortable with the idea that students can learn the content outside class (if they are told what to read or do). Part of this paradigm shift includes the instructor's learning to resist lecturing—by responding to student questions with questions and getting them to explain their thinking. For the expert professional who is teaching in a professional school or program, this is one of the biggest challenges: withholding a direct approach to just answer a question or tell the class what the answer is. This can be difficult for many of us, who can experience a great deal of pleasure from being the expert and having students expect us to pontificate on a moment's notice.

TBL instructors learn to craft the objectives and advanced preparation materials after they have written the team application activities, thereby ensuring a tight fit between preparation and potential success with the most challenging component of the module. With TBL, the Socratic method of exploring students' thinking using questioning becomes the mainstay of the process, for which students are forever grateful. A key to the success of TBL is the instructor-specified objectives for the module and how the instructor specifies the necessary advanced preparation.

In Their Own Words: How the TBL Process Develops Professional Competencies

The development of specific exit competencies in students is at the heart of professional education. In this section, we review several of the key components of TBL and note how each supports the development of these competencies. We also include comments by students that describe how they experienced the various components of TBL. These comments illustrate the power of the components, individually and collectively. (The comments are from student focus group transcripts and course evaluations at Boonshoft School of Medicine, Wright State University, from 2005 to 2007.)

Team Composition. In TBL, three principles should guide the instructor in creating teams: never use student-selected teams, spread the wealth of resources across teams (for example, students' experience, ethnic diversity, skills, attitudes), and make the selection process transparent. When students learn that their assignment to a team is based on a principle of resource wealth distribution, they value their team members from two perspectives: "we are all pretty equal, and we each may have some particular strength to bring to the discussions." Here is a student's description of how one instructor put teams together:

> Right from the start, we knew this class would be different. Prof X said we would be working in teams, but, they would not be self-select. She gave everyone a five-minute five-question math quiz and didn't allow calculators. They were really hard questions, and only a few of us could answer them in our heads, so to speak. She lined us up by our scores, and we counted off to get our team assignment. Cool. Every team got at least one person who could do higher-order math without a calculator. Most of us got none or one correct.

In the workplace, employees rarely get to select with whom they will work with. Nevertheless, team formation in undergraduate courses can still be a contentious issue for students (and therefore instructors). Students often suggest using student-selected teams, but Brickell, Porter, Reynolds, and Cosgrove (1994) suggest that student-selected teams are often just "social entities" and show that these teams underperform when compared to instructor-selected teams. We do the students no favors when we accommodate their desire for student-selected teams. During the application activity phase, the teams come to rely on this diversity of knowledge, skills, and attitudes and the richness it brings to the problem-solving process. The appreciation of the importance of diversity within a team and the strength it brings to the decision-making process is an important realization for students.

Grades. Many educational programs struggle with the goal of helping students become adult learners. Larry Michaelsen learned early that students work more productively and display the attributes of adult learners when proper incentives and assessment structures are present. The impor-

NEW DIRECTIONS FOR TEACHING AND LEARNING • DOI: 10.1002/tl

tant principle in designing assessment practices and instruction in TBL is to emphasize the importance of teamwork. If students have a sense of buy-in on the importance of the dynamic of teamwork, they will work harder and more productively in team activities.

Students at most professional schools come from competitive backgrounds, and initially they are unnerved by the prospect that their individual performance in TBL does not "count" as much as their team's productivity for their own grade. It is important to align the grading practices with the goal of getting the teams to become adult learners. We can achieve this goal by encouraging them to work well and productively together, ensure that teammates come to class prepared, put personality issues aside, and participate fully in the problem-solving process.

These shifts in the classroom can be viewed by students as changes in the rules of engagement and should be thoughtfully presented to students so they understand the rationales and benefits of the TBL approach. Engaging the students in a whole-class decision-making process on the development of the grading structure can send a powerful message that their instructors are working to develop their students' skills and competencies for future careers. Students at this level, initially surprised by the invitation, embrace this offer and buy in to the TBL process—for example:

> This was a real shocker. The whole class had to decide proportional weights for each of the TBL parts, within a range. Never before has a teacher asked for our input on what should count more or less. We had a couple of team members that had been in a TBL course before. They convinced us, and the rest of class, to minimize the grade weight for individual work. With the minimized grade weight of the individual work, we all had to work harder for the group weight!

Readiness Assurance. For instructors, the readiness assurance tests (RATs) can be a highly rewarding experience. The students come to class on time and prepared, When they start the team readiness assurance test (tRAT), the whole class becomes animated, and the ground is being set for the harder group application questions to follow. By moving around the classroom during the gRAT and listening, the instructor can quickly identify misconceptions or gaps in knowledge in the class, but often they are addressed within the teams. This student described the process:

> As soon as the clock struck the hour, we took our iRATs [individual readiness assurance tests] for fifteen minutes. Everyone came on time and was serious. As soon as we turned in our answers and began the tRAT, all hell broke loose as we argued over many of the questions within our teams, but mostly we learned what we didn't know from our peers. I sometimes felt gypped that the professor didn't do a lecture when the class started, but doesn't matter—we learned what we had to learn. Lectures are overrated.

NEW DIRECTIONS FOR TEACHING AND LEARNING • DOI: 10.1002/tl

Professionals in the workplace must not only come prepared and ready to contribute, but also need the ability to teach themselves to meet challenges in the professional practice. In a TBL course, responsibility for learning shifts from the instructor to the team and ultimately the individual student. This shift begins to happen during preparation for the readiness assurance process. Students are required to teach themselves, and during the testing phase they get prompt and unambiguous feedback on the quality of their preparation.

Many other important professional competencies are engaged in the readiness assurance process: the competencies of punctuality, communication, collaboration, consensus decision making, and respect for minority opinion are all of special importance. The structure of the readiness assurance process ensures that these competencies are important. In the professional school curriculum where covering the infinite amount of content is impossible, students soon grasp that just mastering a body of knowledge is not enough; they must go beyond it and often in great depth—an important lesson in self-directed learning for their future professional roles.

> [The professor] gave us the learning objectives and assignments for each TBL module at the beginning of the course. The only two surprises were that they really matched what we did and learned in the module, and to contribute the most in your team, you had to go beyond the minimum in the assignment. I've never worked so hard in a course in my life; I wanted our team to rule.

Group Application. The culmination experience during each module for faculty and students is the group application experience. Often the teams explain their solutions well, and the instructor's work has then been accomplished through the careful design of the module and the facilitation of student discourse. For the instructor, this component can provide an expertise opportunity because the instructor may have to point out the most practical solution to students who do not have the benefit of the instructor's experience or expertise:

> We usually couldn't wait to get to this part because the answers would never be in the book or on the Internet. You had to interpret some data and make a hard decision. Then it was tough to hear from another team how they approached the question—they made more sense and our argument wouldn't hold up. But sometimes, we'd think we were on the right track; one of us would stand up and make the case. What a thrill when the class would clap. We got it!

The solving of complex, multidimensional, poorly defined problems in diverse teams of people is an integral part of the professional workplace. The TBL application activity phase allows students to practice not only their problem-solving skills, but their interpersonal communication and critical thinking skills. It is important that instructors scaffold the development of students' discourse and problem-solving skills, first by letting them practice their discourse in smaller team settings and later in the more public venue of the whole class. The development of these important skills is essential for their later success in the professional workplace. Many competencies are simultaneously addressed within the context of the delivery of the application activities: preparation that goes beyond the minimum, communication, problem solving often with ambiguous data, and team consensus decision making. Many of these competencies are first engaged in the readiness assurance process and are reinforced and further developed in the application activity phase.

Peer Evaluation. It is important that instructors help students learn how to provide constructive feedback that is appropriate for a particular setting. Using the peer evaluation process in TBL and providing specific instruction on making feedback helpful, we can help our students develop these important competencies. When students learn how to evaluate their peers honestly and give constructive feedback, they will likely succeed more readily in the workplace. Students sometimes need to be coached in the skills of providing helpful constructive feedback. Many TBL practitioners use the Michaelsen and Schultheiss article, "Making Feedback Helpful" (1989), to help their students develop their constructive feedback skills.

Accountability is one of the keys to success with team-based learning. Accountability among teammates, in both the classroom and workplace, can be implicit and explicit. In the classroom, the implicit sense of duty to teammates can be fostered during team activities, provided the activities are carefully designed to foster team cohesiveness by requiring preclass preparation, creating opportunities for participation and interdependence. The idea that teams are very good at some tasks and not as good at others is a valuable realization that can help students to excel in the workplace.

There have been some interesting developments recently in the TBL community on the use of peer evaluation. Yost and Lane (2007) now lets their students select the criteria that the teams will use to evaluate each other. The selection of criteria by the students creates a stronger buy-in for the peer evaluation process and makes the criteria for a good performance very explicit to students. A similar method is now being piloted at the University of British Columbia's Mechanical Engineering department (P. Ostafichuk, personal communication, May 2008). Recently Koles, Stolfi, and Parmelee (2008), at Wright State Medical School, has introduced qualitative assessment of student comments, hoping to help students develop their skills in providing constructive feedback. Here is how one student characterized the effect of this process:

> Our team studied the peer evaluation questions the very first day so that we knew how we were to evaluate each other at the end, knowing that it would count for our grade. I know that I changed my behavior starting that day. I tend to procrastinate and not cover details well, so I really prepped ahead for the first time in my life. I wasn't going to get dinged for this.

NEW DIRECTIONS FOR TEACHING AND LEARNING • DOI: 10.1002/tl

Conclusion

With its history of curricular success and excellent outcomes for both students and instructors, TBL is a good fit for professional education. For learners, TBL ensures mastery of core content in the defined domain, engages students in solving progressively complex problems, requires development of interpersonal and communication skills essential for the workplace, and inspires critical thinking skills for making decisions as an individual and within a team. For instructors, it is a strategy that energizes a classroom with dialogue and debate by requiring them to ask, "How did you get to that conclusion?" rather than stating, "Let me tell you the way it is." TBL's learner-centered perspective and tried-and-true practices can help create practitioners of tomorrow within environments of limited resources, high faculty work loads, and large class settings.

References

Baldwin, T. T., Bedell, M. D., and Johnson, J. L. "The Social Fabric of a Team-Based MBA Program: Network Effects on Student Satisfaction." *Academy of Management Journal,* 1997, *40*(6), 1369–1397

Bligh, D. A. *What's the Use of Lectures?* San Francisco: Jossey-Bass, 2000.

Bransford, J. D. (ed.). *How People Learn.* Washington, D.C.: National Academy Press, 2000.

Brickell, J. L., Porter, D. B., Reynolds, M. F., Cosgrove, R. D. "Assigning Students to Groups for Engineering Design Projects: A Comparison of Five Methods." *Journal of Engineering Education,* 1994, *7,* 259–262.

Dunaway, G. A. "Adaptation of Team Learning to an Introductory Graduate Pharmacology Course." *Teaching and Learning in Medicine,* 2005, *17*(1), 56–62.

Fink, D. L. *Creating Significant Learning Experiences: An Integrated Approach to Designing College Courses.* Hoboken, N.J: Jossey-Bass, 2003.

Flexner, A. *Medical Education in United States and Canada.* New York: Carnegie Foundation, 1910.

Freire, P. *The Pedagogy of the Oppressed.* New York: Continuum International, 2000.

Froese, T. *Team-Based Learning in: Construction Engineering and Management.* Retrieved June 2, 2008, from http://cis.apsc.ubc.ca/wiki/images/7/75/CIVIL400_lessons_learned2.doc.

Govaerts, M.J.B. "Educational Competencies or Education for Professional Competence?" *Medical Education,* 2008, *42,* 234–236.

Haidet, P., and others. "A Controlled Trial of Active Versus Passive Learning Strategies in a Large Group Setting." *Advances in Health Sciences Education,* 2004, *9,* 15–27.

Hung, W., Bailey, J. H., and Jonassen, D. H. "Exploring the Tension of Problem-Based Learning: Insights from Research." In D. S. Knowlton and D. C Sharp (eds.), *Problem-Based Learning in the Information Age.* New Directions in Teaching and Learning, no. 95. San Francisco: Jossey-Bass, 2004.

Hunt, D. P., Haidet, P., Coverdale, J. H., and Richards, B. F. "The Effect of Using Team Learning in an Evidence-Based Medicine Course for Medical Students." *Teaching and Learning in Medicine,* 2003, *15,* 131–139

Johnson, D. W., and Johnson, R. T. *Creative Controversy: Intellectual Challenge in the Classroom.* (3rd ed.) Edina, Minn.: Interaction, 1995.

Johnson, D. W., and Johnson, R. T. *Assessment of Students in Groups.* Thousand Oaks, Calif.: Corwin Press, 2004.

Kelly, P. A., and others. "A Comparison of In-Class Learner Engagement Across Lecture, Problem-Based Learning, and Team Learning Using the STROBE Classroom Observation Tool." *Teaching and Learning in Medicine,* 2005, *17*(2), 112–118.

Koles, P., Stolfi, A., and Parmelee, D. "Impact of Team-Based Learning on Second-Year Medical Students' Performance on Pathology-Based Exam Questions." Abstract presented at the Central Group of Educational Affairs of the American Association of Medical Colleges Annual Meeting, Columbus, Ohio, Apr. 1, 2008.

Koles, P., and others. "Active Learning in a Year 2 Pathology Curriculum." *Journal of Medical Education,* 2005, *39*(10), 1045–1055.

McKeachie, W. J. *Teaching Tips: A Guidebook for the Beginning College Teacher.* (8th ed.) Lexington, Mass.: Heath, 1986.

Michaelsen, L. K., and Schultheiss, E. E. "Making Feedback Helpful." *Journal of Management Education,* 1989, *13*, 109–113.

Michaelsen, L. K., Watson, W. E., and Black, R. H. "A Realistic Test of Individual Versus Group Consensus Decision Making." *Journal of Applied Psychology,* 1989 74(5), 834–839.

Nieder, G. L., Parmelee, D. X., Stolfi, A., and Hudes, P. D. "Team-Based Learning in a Medical Gross Anatomy and Embryology Course." *Clinical Anatomy,* 2005, *18,* 56–63.

Ostafichuk, P. M., and Hodgson, A. J. *Team-Based Learning in: Mechanical Design.* 2005. Retrieved June 2, 2008, from http://cis.apsc.ubc.ca/wiki/images/6/65/Mech2_lessons_learned.doc.

Ryan, T. E. "What Textbook Reading Teaches Students." *Teaching Professor.* 2008. Retrieved Mar. 28, 2008, from http://www.magnapubs.com/teachingprofessor/.

Searle, N. S., and others. "TBL in Medical Education: Initial Experiences at Ten Institutions." *Academic Medicine,* 2003, 78(10 Suppl.), S55–58.

Vasan, N. S., and DeFouw, D. "Team Learning in a Medical Gross Anatomy Course." *Journal of Medical Education,* 2005, *39*(5), 524.

Weeks, W. "Incorporation of Active Learning Strategies in the Engineering Classroom." Paper presented at the ASEE Midwest Section Meeting, University of Missouri-Rolla, Sept. 2003.

Yost, S. A., and Lane, D. R. "Implementing a Problem-Based Multi-Disciplinary Civil Engineering Design Capstone: Evolution, Assessment, and Lessons Learned with Industry Partners." Paper presented at the American Society for Engineering Education Southeastern Section Annual Conference, Louisville, Ky., 2007.

JIM SIBLEY is director of the Centre for Instructional Support in the Faculty of Applied Science at the University of British Columbia, Canada.

DEAN X. PARMELEE is associate dean for Academic Affairs at the Wright State University Boonshoft School of Medicine and a professor of psychiatry and pediatrics.

This chapter describes the teaching competencies, facilitation strategies, and personal characteristics that minimize student frustration, increase the fidelity of TBL implementation, and ultimately moderate student success.

Teaching Skills for Facilitating Team-Based Learning

Derek R. Lane

Taken together, the chapters in this volume demonstrate that team-based learning (TBL) is a unique student-centered instructional strategy that emphasizes learning to use concepts rather than merely learning about them. As such, TBL requires students to become active participants who are accountable and responsible for their learning. This does not occur, however, unless teachers transform their primary role from a sage dispenser of knowledge to a more sophisticated guide, course designer, and manager of the overall instructional process.

My experience as an advocate for and trainer of TBL for almost fifteen years is that when instructors possess the necessary teaching competencies and carefully implement the defining principles of TBL as outlined in Chapter One and the appendix at the end of the volume, students are better prepared, more engaged, and more likely to acquire knowledge that facilitates lifelong learning. In addition, when students willingly share in the responsibility to ensure that learning occurs, teaching is simply more fun because students begin to behave more like colleagues. Unfortunately, incomplete or inadequate implementation may result in negative experiences, student resistance, or some combination of feelings of indignation, frustration, and general distaste for the process. Therefore, the focus of this chapter is on the teaching competencies, facilitation strategies, and personal characteristics that minimize student frustration, increase the fidelity of TBL implementation, and ultimately moderate student success.

NEW DIRECTIONS FOR TEACHING AND LEARNING, no. 116, Winter 2008 © Wiley Periodicals, Inc.
Published online in Wiley InterScience (www.interscience.wiley.com) • DOI: 10.1002/tl.333

55

Teaching Competencies

Effective implementation of TBL is dependent on the communication skills and techniques of the instructor. Many advocates of team-based learning, including me, will argue that the majority of experienced teachers already have most of the skills required to implement team-based learning effectively. Knowledgeable teachers have learned how to organize material around instructional objectives, create and give tests and assignments, and provide feedback on student performance. The major change, which can be a difficult one, is thinking differently about what should be happening in the classroom. Instead of thinking about how we should be teaching, we have to focus on what we can do to enhance student learning. Teaching competencies for team-based learning need to expand to include strategies for guiding and encouraging students to articulate their understanding of the course content.

The essential skills required to use team-based learning effectively include the ability to create a climate for student-centered learning, respond to individual student needs, and guide learners through their own discovery by asking open-ended questions as they engage in reflective dialogue and critical thinking. Facilitation skills are also paramount. A TBL instructor's goal is to guide the groups, facilitate their growth, and manage the classroom environment without getting in the way of student learning. Because of their importance, between-group facilitation strategies are presented separately. The other new skill that appears to provide the greatest challenge to new team learning users is developing the ability to design effective group assignments, which requires imaginative management in the creation of purposeful tasks that result in meaningful application of course content. A thorough discussion of designing effective group assignments goes beyond the scope of this chapter, but the strategies have been summarized elsewhere (Michaelsen, Fink, and Knight, 1997; Michaelsen and Sweet, 2008).

Creating a Climate for Student-Centered Learning. Instructors are encouraged to maintain an open mind and a willingness to accept new ideas. This is the prerequisite to creating an inclusive environment so that students quickly become active participants in the learning community. It is also important to guide students in developing a positive attitude toward the learning process and group work by formulating and communicating clear and specific expectations. Let students know that TBL works best when everyone works together to build trust, cooperation, support, and mutual respect. Students will not contribute to a discussion if they are worried that they will be ridiculed or criticized by the instructor or other students. Achieving student commitment and building individual accountability is accomplished with teacher enthusiasm and modeling.

Laying the groundwork for team-based learning begins on the first day. Students need to understand what the course will require them to learn and how it will relate to other work, why TBL is being used and how the class will be conducted (What will be the work load? What types of exams are given? How will grades be determined?), and something about the personality of the teacher (What kind of person is the teacher going to be? Will the teacher be easily accessible? Will the teacher be easy to talk with?). The instructor must be knowledgeable, confident, and enthusiastic about TBL throughout the academic term in order to encourage the development of positive group norms. Instructors should spend time at the beginning of the course describing appropriate group dynamics, specific expectations about respectful collaboration, and the value of open and honest discussion. They need to make certain that all students understand that decisions should be a group process, not just the decisions by the most self-assured and outspoken members. Positive expectations will yield positive results.

Student Resistance. Challenge behavior is a natural consequence of group dynamics. That is, when students are arranged in small groups, student resistance increases because there is strength in numbers and students will ask questions (and challenge the instructor) in a group when they would not engage in such behavior as separate individuals. As challenge behavior increases, student interaction also increases. The key to managing challenge behavior is to understand the source of the resistance and to use positive and productive strategies that encourage student commitment and simultaneously establish instructor credibility. The two most prominent sources of student resistance experienced by instructors using TBL are concerns that students have about grades (especially group and helping behavior grades) and concerns that students are teaching themselves. Student concerns about grades can be alleviated using a grade weighting assignment that increases student acceptance of and commitment to the grading process (see Michaelsen, Cragin, and Watson, 1981; Michaelsen, Knight, and Fink, 2004).

Student Perceptions That They Are "Teaching Themselves." When TBL is working well, students genuinely enjoy the process of working in groups and engaging in application-oriented activities. And because instructors rarely have to discuss basic concepts or answer simple questions, they enjoy a sense of renewed energy and satisfaction with teaching because students are behaving less like "empty vessels" and more like colleagues. However, if students believe they are teaching themselves (as opposed to becoming willing partners who share responsibility to ensure that learning occurs), the TBL process will increasingly frustrate them. There are several possible causes for this "we are teaching ourselves" perception. The first occurs when novice TBL instructors simply replace their lectures with a series of individual and group readiness assessment tests without allowing students the opportunity to adequately engage the content and apply it in meaningful ways. A good rule of thumb is to include no fewer than four and no more than seven individual and group readiness assessment tests during the academic term (each corresponding to the major units of instruction in TBL).

The perception that students are teaching themselves can also occur when instructors provide too many assigned readings—or, worse, the wrong kinds of readings, confusing or dense ones, for example, that

NEW DIRECTIONS FOR TEACHING AND LEARNING • DOI: 10.1002/tl

require students to dedicate countless hours of study to memorize intricate details, then to be tested only on general concepts. A third cause is poorly designed readiness assessment tests that are too long, too detailed, or not reflective of what students have read and learned. (Comprehensive information about how to design effective readiness assessment tests is readily available elsewhere. See Michaelsen, Watson, and Shrader, 1985; Michaelsen, Knight, and Fink, 2004.) Students will become discouraged and frustrated if the TBL instructor is unavailable or frequently leaves the classroom during the application-oriented activities. Instructors should be present and monitor group progress. Finally, students may feel like as if are teaching themselves because TBL instructors do not transmit content through formal lectures; this is especially annoying to students who have developed unfortunate habits of passive reception.

Maintaining Credibility Without Excessive Lecturing. Instructors can establish their credibility as content experts through guided questions, instructor feedback, and limited full-class discussions while allowing students multiple opportunities to engage and apply the content in enjoyable ways. As we establish credibility, students learn that they are not on their own and that there is value-added because we are guiding them through the instructional process. One strategy that allows the instructor to establish credibility, which should be incorporated only before the first readiness assessment test, is to engage students by asking a few direct open-ended questions and allowing them to ask limited clarification questions before they complete their first individual readiness assessment test. This strategy allows instructors to prime student thinking about the essentials of the preclass readings and build credibility. Keep in mind that in almost all cases, instructors should avoid giving students information that they can and should obtain through the preclass readings.

The instructor feedback that occurs immediately after the appeals process provides additional opportunities to clarify student confusion, offers evidence of personal expertise, and frames examples so that students can successfully synthesize the knowledge gained in the team application assignments. There will also be times when students will require additional clarification or examples. Rather than repeat the content to each individual group, instructors can engage the entire class in a brief discussion to clarify some of the major issues that will allow students to make specific connections among the concepts.

Responding to Individual Student Needs. Teacher behavior can have an enormous effect on how groups function. Jaques (2003) argues that teachers who talk too much or who give a lecture rather than conducting a dialogue can interfere with group development and student learning. Being an effective TBL instructor involves making the right sort of nudges and interventions, but it also means knowing when (if at all) and how to intervene. Instructors need to think about how to empower students rather than control them by teaching the joy of learning through discovery. It is therefore critical that instructors monitor the timing and type of their interactions with the individual teams. TBL provides a strong and stable structure, especially when readiness assurance tests and immediate feedback assessment techniques are used appropriately, so that frequent interventions are not necessary. When students can clearly see how team projects are relevant and prepare them for advanced course work, and ultimately, professional life, most are more enthusiastic about team-based learning. The nature of the readiness assurance process in team-based learning demands out-of-class individual student preparation and serves to reinforce student collaboration. As a result, students rarely come to class unprepared. When they do, the combination of a low individual readiness assessment test score, along with peer pressure from teammates, is enough to discourage future infractions. Attendance is seldom a problem for the same reasons. Students benefit most when they manage group dynamics without the aid of the instructor.

Guiding Learners Through Their Own Discovery. The goal of the TBL instructor is to guide the groups, facilitate their growth, and manage the classroom environment without getting in the way of student learning. In order to accomplish this goal, instructors should integrate within-group facilitation strategies to prime the pump before they incorporate between-group facilitation techniques to keep student discovery, interaction, and learning flowing. In order to assist students in their efforts to engage in reflective dialogue and critical thinking, instructors must prepare any necessary materials, explain and check agreement on the tasks to be accomplished—as well as the deliverable outcomes, monitor the development of the tasks, and control the time boundaries.

Using Within-Group Strategies to Prime the Pump. During the initial instructional activity sequence, it is necessary for the instructor to continually monitor the progress of each group. Circulating around the room as the students are working lets them know that we care about what they are doing— and that they are not teaching themselves. Guide students to do their own reasoning by asking open-ended questions to keep them focused on the issues and promote more complex thinking. Keep the learning process moving by having students talk, discuss, and argue among themselves about the issues and the most appropriate strategy for applying the content to make a decision.

Gelula (1997) suggests that instructors can best guide learners through their own discovery by focusing on discussion that clarifies information and concepts, raising levels of student involvement, asking questions that lead students to more complex thinking strategies, and using the group strength to develop decision making skills. Jaques (2000, 2003) advises that when instructors present a question they do not answer it themselves or try to reformulate it. Instructors should count to ten silently before speaking again. And when instructors have something that they could say (which could be most of the time), they should count to ten again. If a group is polarized around two possible solutions, asking students to introduce a third solution to the discussion will eliminate the perception that one of the initial two solutions is correct. If a group is having difficulties progressing, it is beneficial to ask students to provide examples of their thinking. The value of effective within-group management to prime the pump of student discovery when using team-based learning should not be underestimated. Equally important, however, are the between-group instructor facilitation strategies that keep the student discovery, interaction, and learning flowing.

Facilitation Strategies

In their chapter focusing on facilitator skills necessary to organize and conduct team-based learning activities, Pelley and McMahon (2008) argue that the most important skill for a facilitator is "the ability to help teams verbalize their rationales during the large-group discussions" (p. 99). Although they provide excellent advice about specific questions and scenarios that can be used to elicit student justifications (for example, "Tell me about your thinking." "Did anyone have a close second choice?" "What would make this answer correct?" "Can anyone add to this?"), their advice is incomplete. TBL facilitators must not only possess excellent questioning skills that will focus classroom conversations, but must also be able to provide positive feedback for participation, require that students summarize key points raised in the discussion, and ultimately facilitate student learning through critical reflection.

The single best way to gauge the effectiveness of group assignments is to observe the level of energy that is present when the results of the small group discussions are reported to the class as a whole. Instructors who are new to TBL may inadvertently create a hostile and adversarial environment when they first attempt to facilitate large group student discussions. The key to successful facilitation is not to promote competition between the teams, but rather to encourage student-centered critical reflection and comparison in an atmosphere of genuine mutual respect.

To achieve optimal results with team-based learning, facilitators are required to be good question askers—asking open-ended questions to promote complex thinking and closed-ended questions only when specific information is needed to advance the discussion. We have already established that students learn best when they are actively involved and that student experiences provide the basis for discussion. TBL facilitators need to be flexible and integrate student responses into the discussion. When facilitating a dialogue with students, instructors should keep in mind the purpose of the discussion, carefully plan how they will conduct each session, discuss their expectations and reinforce them throughout the course, and avoid closed-ended questions that require yes or no answers.

Focusing Conversations Using a Four-Stage Process. The solution to the problems inherent in facilitating a dialogue with students is to focus the conversation. Stanfield (2000) presents a relatively simple four-stage process for focusing critical reflection that begins with objective-level questions (for example, about facts and external reality perceived by group members), moves to reflective-level questions (for example, about personal reactions and internal responses to the data), continues with questions at the interpretive level (for example, that draw out meaning, values, significance, and implications), and concludes with decisional-level questions (for example, to elicit resolution, bring the conversation to a close, and allow the groups to make a resolve about the future as it relates to the discussion). The process is referred to for short as ORID (Objective, Reflective, Interpretive, and Decisional).

The basic model for an ORID summary technique employed after the first instructional activity sequence in team-based learning begins with an opening statement to frame the discussion, followed by objective, reflective, interpretive, and decisional questions, and ending with a closing statement. For example, an instructor might begin the discussion with an opening statement: "Before we move on to the next instructional unit, it is important to reflect on what we learned in this unit. We need to look back at our experiences. So let's take a few minutes to reflect on what we've just done. I'm very interested in how it went. Do you mind talking about it?" The instructor would then begin by asking a series of questions that are appropriately sequenced. It is critical that instructors give students sufficient time to think about and answer the questions. Being comfortable in the silence and waiting more than five seconds before moving to another question is an important part of the ORID process.

Objective Questions. Examples of objective questions include these:

"What parts of this application assignment really caught your attention?"
"What specific words, phrases, or images still linger in your mind?"
"What do you remember from the application?"
"What were some of the key events for you in this past unit?"
"What words or phrases did you hear in the team reports?"
"Which parts came through very clearly for you?"
"What parts were unclear?"
"What did we get done?"
"What use is being made of your skills and time?"
"What information stood out for you?"
"If you were a reporter, how would you report in a sentence what happened?"

Reflective Questions. Once the conversation has been framed and students are comfortable answering the objective questions, it is necessary to advance the discussion by asking a series of reflective questions—for example:

"What is the mood of your group as you work? Excitement? Frustration?"
"What were the demands and pressures you faced on this project? What has been the most difficult for you?"
"What were the high points of the application for you?"
"Where did you feel most challenged?"
"Where did you turn off?"

"What part of the process left you skeptical or frustrated?" "Where were you
   frustrated?"
"What was your biggest surprise?"
"Where did you have a breakthrough?"
"What is going really well?"
"Where have you seen ways you can improve?"
"What are the key values being emphasized in this TBL curriculum?"
"Which parts are you concerned about?"
"How has this process affected you personally?"
"How has it affected how your group works?"

It is not necessary to ask all of the questions, but rather to ensure that
students have a sufficient context (based on what they remember and how
they felt about the course content and process) before answering the more
salient interpretive questions.

Interpretive Questions. By the time instructors begin asking interpretive
questions, students should be relaxed and ready to contribute to a more sub-
stantive discussion of what they have learned. Examples of interpretive
questions are:

"What were the key learning lessons from the application?"
"How has the unit been beneficial to you?"
"How has it met your expectations?"
"What did we learn from things that went well in the group?"
"What did we learn from the times when the group struggled?"
"If you were going to do the application again, what, if anything, would you
   do differently?"
"Where is a breakthrough needed?"
"What will enable your group to move forward? How might you person-
   ally help?"
"How are you and your group personally different after working with and
   learning to use this content?"
"What questions or issues do we need to work through as a group?
"What are your reflections on what happened?"

Since the primary focus of TBL is helping students to use and apply
course content, instructors need to help students make conscious decisions
about how to incorporate what they have learned in future interactions by
asking decisional questions.

Decisional Questions. Instructors might begin asking decisional questions such as, "What is the next step in making certain that we can improve
how we learn and apply course content? What resources do you think you'll
need?" or "What are you going to do next?" It is beneficial to ask students,
"How can I help?" so that they fully understand that the role of the TBL

instructor is to guide and support student learning. Here are some additional decisional questions:

"What are we saying we want to do differently so that the group works more efficiently?"

"What unfinished business do we need to complete before we can be successful in our future collaborations?"

"What do you recommend that would help you apply more effectively what you have learned?"

"What changes would you suggest? Which of these suggestions is the highest priority?"

"As you reflect on what we have said, what seem to be the next steps?"

A Concluding ORID Conversation. Finally, an ORID conversation should conclude with a supportive statement that summarizes the discussion and encourages future dialogue—for example:

> You have all done excellent work reflecting on the process. I've gained some new insights into our experience, as I'm certain we all have. This has been a great discussion and a significant step in our journey. I trust you've all noticed how quickly we moved from learning about concepts to learning to use them. This has been very helpful to us all in getting the big picture and seeing where we need to move next. I'm very interested to see how we can implement what we learned to be even more successful as the course progresses. Thank you for your contributions and sharing with honesty.

The incorporation of the ORID model when facilitating TBL activities allows all students to become active participants in the dialogue. Objective and reflective questions are open ended and do not require one correct answer. Interpretive and decisional-level questions are also open ended but serve to focus the conversation and facilitate student learning through critical reflection. In addition to providing positive verbal and nonverbal feedback throughout the discussion, TBL facilitators must solicit student responses that synthesize and summarize the key points raised during the discussion. These summary statements are made by students but should tie directly back to the goals and objectives associated with the specific instructional activity sequence. Facilitation skills can be developed with increased effort and practice.

Active Listening as an Important Facilitation Strategy. Another valuable instructor facilitation strategy is active listening. Instructors who successfully incorporate active listening into classroom dialogues find that students are not only more willing to participate but also more committed to and excited about team-based learning. Active listening provides essential feedback to students that what they are saying and learning is of great consequence to the instructor. Several key instructor behaviors are necessary for active listening to be effective:

- Listening to the content as well as the emotional meaning underlying the student's statements
- Assessing the student's nonverbal communication
- Monitoring personal nonverbal and emotional filters
- Listening to the student nonjudgmentally and with empathy, using restatements, paraphrasing, and probing as clarifying tactics

Listening to Factual Content and Personal Intent. When a student is answering a question, instructors need to make eye contact with him or her and suspend other things they might be doing. Instructors must listen to what the student is saying in terms of facts and ideas. When instructors listen to the content of the student comments as well as the emotional intent of the messages, they are more likely to give supportive feedback by sending appropriate verbal and nonverbal messages that communicate sincere interest in what the student is saying. In addition, it is important to listen to the emotional meaning underlying what the student is saying. If the student is frustrated or seems defensive, it is imperative that the instructor remains calm and does not respond defensively.

Assessing Student Nonverbal Communication. It is also necessary for the TBL instructor to read and interpret the student's body language and other nonverbal signals that may communicate more about whether a student has learned to apply the course concepts or is still struggling with basic content knowledge or other issues. Students who are engaged in the TBL learning process will have increased vocal variety, movement, and gestures; smiles and nods; eye contact; and a relaxed body posture.

Monitoring Instructor Personal Nonverbal and Emotional Filters. Students who are anxious or defensive have the potential to create a hostile TBL environment. The most important preventive strategy for dealing with student challenge behavior is for instructors to be aware of the nonverbal messages they might be sending as they react to student resistance. The key is giving feedback appropriate for the situation and offering it in a way that assists the TBL process and student learning. Instructors need to be aware of their own feelings and strong opinions. When they are cognizant of the emotional filters that affect their understanding of and reactions to student resistance, they quickly realize that 99.9 percent of all negative occurrences in any TBL classroom are directly related to the instructor and how student resistance is managed. One of the best strategies to dealing with student resistance is to listen to the student nonjudgmentally and with empathy.

Listening to the Student Nonjudgmentally and with Empathy. Instructors who put themselves in the student's shoes and understand what is shaping her or his feelings are especially successful in their attempts to manage student resistance. It is critical that instructors not prejudge students; rather, they

NEW DIRECTIONS FOR TEACHING AND LEARNING • DOI: 10.1002/tl

should restate, paraphrase, and ask additional probing questions that may clarify meanings and reveal underlying issues and potential barriers to learning.

Using Clarifying Tactics in Active Listening. Instructors who incorporate clarifying tactics as part of their facilitation strategies can be confident that they are using active listening effectively as part of the TBL process. For example, they might seek to clarify meanings with questions such as, "I hear you saying you are frustrated with factorial analyses, Pat. Is that right?" In addition, instructors may ask students, "Tell me more about a specific time when your group had a breakthrough," as a way to probe student thoughts and feelings about how course concepts are being applied. Instructors may also encourage elaboration by asking students to talk about "what happened next" or "how that made you feel."

It is important that instructors not attempt to complete student statements. Instead, they should ask questions that encourage discovery, for example, "What do you feel were the possible alternative solutions to the application activity?" and clarification questions such as, "What did you mean when you said that the group process affected you personally?" Throughout the active listening process, instructors should check their tone for sincerity and continue to ask open-ended questions that foster a variety of responses.

Remember that the purpose of active listening is to show interest in the student and the conversation by asking sincere, nondirective questions such as, "Tell me more about that" or "Keep going, I'm following you." Whenever possible, instructors should use students' own words and use signposts such as, "May I repeat back to you my understanding of what you just said so I do not get it wrong?"

Paraphrasing. Restating a student's message in a way that sounds natural can be a difficult skill to master. Paraphrasing is feedback that restates, in the words of the instructor, the message he or she thought the student sent. There are three approaches to incorporating paraphrasing in team-based learning: changing the student's wording ("Let me see if I've got this right. You're confused about . . . ?"), offering an example of what the instructor thinks the student is talking about ("You think those two-way interaction effects were difficult to interpret, so you omitted them from your analyses?"), and reflecting the underlying theme of the student's remarks ("You keep reminding me that the members of your team like each other and that you work well together. It sounds as if you are worried that you may be wasting time during some of your group work sessions?"). Paraphrasing is an excellent way to take the heat out of intense discussions ("Okay. Let me be sure I understand you. It sounds like you're concerned about . . ."). Paraphrasing is also effective for managing student challenge behavior because it ensures the students of their instructor's involvement and concern. When instructors take the time to restate and clarify a student's message, their commitment to listening is hard to deny. TBL instructors need to remember that paraphrasing involves feedback of both factual information and personal information. Using ORID and active listening will help build teacher-student relationships and ensure that students will not feel trapped or grilled during a TBL dialogue.

Personal Instructor Characteristics

Regardless of the teaching approach that instructors use, the personal characteristics of any teacher have both positive and negative impacts on student learning. For optimal results using TBL, instructors should be knowledgeable, flexible, spontaneous, and confident with the team-based learning process. They need not be flawless with the process, but there are some important instructor characteristics that are beneficial to the successful implementation of team-based learning.

When designing a TBL course, instructors must ensure that their knowledge extends beyond course content expertise to include an understanding of how the course is aligned with the curriculum, how to assess whether students comprehend and are able to apply the course content, and how the content is relevant to students. In addition, they should be patient, flexible, spontaneous, and able to anticipate potential problems and remove barriers when possible.

It is critical that instructors be confident enough with the TBL instructional activity sequence and readiness assurance process that they can avoid common traps. Instructors should take care that they do not eliminate necessary components (individual or group readiness assurance tests, formative or summative peer evaluations, the five-minute rule [being told when there is five minutes left within which to complete a test]), add detrimental assignments (group papers, too many take-home assessment tests), or ignore recommendations about openly forming groups that will remain permanent throughout the academic term. Another important point is that instructors should avoid the need for students to complete the application assignments outside regular class sessions. Finally, instructors need to be comfortable with student challenge behavior and enjoy the increased student interaction.

One of the primary sources of student frustration with TBL relates to personal instructor characteristics that are counterproductive and establish conditions under which team-based learning is less effective:

- *Deficient content expertise.* This condition involves the novice instructor who has not yet mastered the course content. Novice teachers typically rely heavily on a textbook to organize instruction and thus tend to stay only one chapter ahead of their students. When students ask questions that go beyond the reading—questions that a novice teacher is unable to answer—the instructor loses credibility and jeopardizes the successful implementation of TBL.
- *Teacher-centered focus.* Although the TBL instructor is always the content expert and should never relinquish this role, the impact of team-based learning is limited in the second condition where instructors are unwilling or unable to relinquish their instructional power as expert lecturers—

and thus prevent their transformation into classroom guides. Instructors who possess this personal characteristic also believe that losing control and allowing students to work in teams will result in the sharing of incorrect assumptions and understandings. This concern, however, is dependent on a narrow, and largely inaccurate, view of teaching as simple transmission. Research clearly demonstrates that increased student engagement and involvement are necessary for deep learning to occur. Just because we teach something does not mean that students have learned it. Conversely, because this group of teachers very much enjoys preparing and presenting lectures as a central performing aspect of teaching, it is doubtful that TBL will turn out well for them. Put simply, team-based learning is a student-centered instructional strategy that is unsuitable for exclusive teacher-centered approaches to instruction.

- *Anxiety and defensiveness.* The third condition under which TBL should not be used includes instructors who feel threatened by frequent student challenges, especially when the challenges come from students who are united in groups. Team-based learning fosters student engagement and increases challenge behavior. Instructors who are unable to effectively manage the increased interaction tend to react defensively, and students become frustrated.

- *No clarity about content application.* The desire for knowledge for its own sake is a lofty goal, but the use of team-based learning by instructors who are not confident about what they want students to do—beyond memorization—with the course content is a colossal mistake. The principal component of team-based learning is that it requires instructors to provide opportunities to students for learning how to apply basic course concepts in meaningful ways and to reward them. Instructors who fail to incorporate significant application-focused assignments will almost certainly experience unenthusiastic student reactions to team-based learning.

- *Insufficient time for course redesign.* Restructuring a traditional course for team-based learning, creating readiness assessment tests, developing effective application-focused team assignments, and designing an appropriate TBL grading system require that instructors invest a significant amount of time before students arrive for their first day of class. Team-based learning requires that courses be organized, clear, relevant, and prepared in advance. Instructors who are unable to invest the time needed to redesign their approach to teaching are cautioned against using team-based learning.

Students in TBL courses learn more, are much more prepared, and are better able to engage in lifelong learning. They simply need to understand that they are not doing it on their own. Student complaints and resistance can be minimized when students know that the course is relevant, the instructor is credible, and what they are learning ultimately matters. Student success therefore is moderated by the teaching competencies, facilitation strategies, and the personal characteristics of TBL instructors.

Perhaps the greatest benefit of TBL is that it has a tremendous positive impact on the instructor because it enlivens the classroom and makes teaching more fun, energizing, and nonrepetitive. Implementing the teaching skills for facilitating team-based learning identified in this chapter should translate into more meaningful positive experiences for both students and instructors.

References

Gelula, M. H. "Clinical Discussion Sessions and Small Groups." *Surgical Neurology,* 1997, *47,* 399–402.

Jaques, D. *Learning in Groups.* London: Kogan Page, 2000.

Jaques, D. "ABC of Learning and Teaching in Medicine: Teaching Small Groups." *BMJ,* 2003, *326,* 492–494.

Michaelsen, L. K., Cragin, J. P., and Watson, W. E. "Grading and Anxiety: A Strategy for Coping." *Organizational Behavior Teaching Journal,* 1981, *6,* 8–14.

Michaelsen, L. K., Fink, L. D., and Knight, A. "Designing Effective Group Activities: Lessons for Classroom Teaching and Faculty Development." In D. DeZure (ed.), *To Improve the Academy.* Stillwater, Okla.: New Forums, 1997.

Michaelsen, L. K., Knight, A. B., and Fink, L. D. (eds.). *Team-Based Learning: A Transformative Use of Small Groups in College Teaching.* Sterling, Va.: Stylus, 2004.

Michaelsen, L. K., and Sweet, M. S. "Fundamental Principles and Practices of Team-Based Learning." In L. K. Michaelsen, D. X. Parmelee, K. K. McMahon, and R. E. Levine (eds.). *Team-Based Learning for Health Professions Education: A Guide to Using Small Groups for Improving Learning.* Sterling, Va.: Stylus, 2008.

Michaelsen, L. K., Watson, W. E., and Shrader, C. B. "Informative Testing: A Practical Approach for Tutoring with Groups." *Organizational Behavior Teaching Review,* 1985, *9,* 18–33.

Pelley, J. W., and McMahon, K. K. "Facilitator Skills." In L. K. Michaelsen, D. X. Parmelee, K. K. McMahon and R. E. Levine (eds.), *Team-Based Learning for Health Professions Education: A Guide to Using Small Groups for Improving Learning.* Sterling, Va.: Stylus, 2008.

Stanfield, R. B. (ed.). *The Art of Focused Conversation: 100 Ways to Access Group Wisdom in the Workplace.* Gabriola Island, B.C.: New Society Publishers, 2000.

DEREK R. LANE *is an associate dean in the College of Communications and Information Studies and associate professor in the Department of Communication at the University of Kentucky.*

This chapter discusses the merits of peer assessment and evaluation; the instructional guidelines, issues, and considerations for their use in the TBL classroom, and a brief description of peer assessment methods and information on how to access forms.

Peer Assessment and Evaluation in Team-Based Learning

Christina M. Cestone, Ruth E. Levine, Derek R. Lane

In contrast to traditional courses, in which students are accountable only to the instructor, effective implementation of any group-based instructional format, including team-based learning (TBL), requires that students be accountable to both the instructor and their peers. Unfortunately, some instructors resist using groups because of concerns about using peer evaluations or poorly designed group assignments and grading systems that in effect reward and encourage social loafing. Furthermore, their concerns seem as equally focused on unfairly raising the grades of poor students (who may be carried along by hard-working members) as they are about the potential of penalizing hard-working students (who may receive a lower course grade because they were randomly assigned to a poorly performing group).

With TBL, however, these concerns are largely eliminated by using a comprehensive feedback and grading system that ensures individual student accountability to both the instructor and peers by using a grading system that has an individual performance component, a team performance component, and a peer evaluation component (Michaelsen, 1992; Michaelsen, Knight, and Fink, 2004; Chapter One, this volume). Individual student grade incentives for accountability in TBL courses are derived from four separate but interrelated sources: individual preparation (scores on the individual readiness assurance test); collective preparation (scores on the team readiness assurance test); how well knowledge is applied by individuals

NEW DIRECTIONS FOR TEACHING AND LEARNING, no. 116, Winter 2008 © Wiley Periodicals, Inc.
Published online in Wiley InterScience (www.interscience.wiley.com) • DOI: 10.1002/tl.334

within a team, as a team, to solve progressively difficult problems (application exercise scores); and contributions to interpersonal group dynamics, team maintenance, cohesion, and team productivity (peer evaluation scores).

Peer assessment and evaluation are essential elements of TBL for two reasons. First, peer assessment provides formative (process) information to help individual students improve team performance over time and develop the interpersonal and team skills essential for their future success. Second, peer evaluation scores provide summative (outcome) data to the instructor that can be used to ensure fairness in grading by incorporating an assessment of each member's contributions to the success of their teams and make judgments about it (Falchikov and Goldfinch, 2000; Topping, Smith, Swanson, and Elliot, 2000; Topping, 2005).

This chapter discusses the pedagogical merits of peer assessment and evaluation as mechanisms for enhancing student accountability and presents the instructional guidelines, issues, and considerations for use in the TBL classroom. It concludes with a brief description of peer assessment methods and information about how to access and use the corresponding forms.

Pedagogical Merits of Peer Assessment and Evaluation

TBL is a unique pedagogical strategy that facilitates the development of a variety of skills relative to future professional pursuits, including individual accountability, problem solving, interpersonal communication, teamwork, and organizational skills (Brindley and Scoffield, 1998; Boud, Cohen, and Sampson, 1999; Butcher et al., cited in Cheng and Warren, 2000; Lane, 2007; Levine, 2008). TBL provides students with multiple and varied opportunities to develop these skills as they engage in team activities including team readiness assurance tests (tRATs), group preparation of written appeals, and application-oriented problem-solving activities and exams (Michaelsen, Knight, and Fink, 2004).

Students also receive a number of benefits from engaging in the process of peer assessment and evaluation. For example, judgment by peers seems to provide a more significant motivator to produce high-quality work than does the assessment of a single instructor (Searby and Ewers, 1997). As a result, when peers are accountable to each other, the time spent comparing work and discussing ideas and concepts in teams is more productive. Put simply, students learn from the cognitive processes of their peers (Brindley and Scoffield, 1998). Furthermore, when students become assessors, they are required to show a more thoughtful understanding of the processes involved in the activity (Searby and Ewers, 1997).

In their meta-analysis of peer assessment studies, Dochy, Segers, and Sluijmans (1999) identified several positive effects of using various peer, self, and coassessment processes to improve the quality of learning. Two of the most prominent were increased confidence in one's performance and increased quality in the learning output. Peer assessment and evaluation also serve to help students take more control over their learning through development of critical analysis of the work of others (Searby and Ewers, 1997). Repeated reading of peer writing, for example, reinforces analysis of one's own work processes and makes the learning more visible to the learner (Topping, Smith, Swanson, and Elliot, 2000). Similarly, music composition students who were responsible for analyzing the compositions of other students were better able to recognize the components of a quality composition against which they could hold their own work (Searby and Ewers, 1997).

Peer assessment is also useful for helping students to scrutinize the purposes and objectives of a course (Smith, Swanson, and Elliot, 2000). When conducted prior to the end of the semester, peer evaluation enabled earlier identification of misunderstandings or gaps in thinking (Searby and Ewers, 1997) that could then be addressed by targeted discussion of specific course content. Finally, peer assessment and evaluation are essential to a comprehensive grading process in TBL because team members are typically the only ones who have enough information to accurately assess one another's contributions (Michaelsen, 2004).

Student Perceptions of Peer Assessment and Evaluation

An examination of the literature across disciplines indicates a range of differences in terms of learner acceptance of peer evaluation. Several studies have demonstrated positive correlations regarding faculty evaluations and written exam performance (Levine, 2008). In some studies, learners expressed satisfaction with and believed they benefited from peer evaluation (Gatfield, 1999; Paswan and Gollakota, 2004), while in others, learners resisted the process. Learners who were accepting of the process believed that the quality of their work improved as a result of the feedback they received (Brindley and Scoffield, 1998; Dochy, Segers, and Sluijmans, 1999; Topping, Smith, Swanson, and Elliot, 2000). Students who disliked peer evaluation believed that the process interfered with the relationships with their fellow learners (Levine, 2008). While some students experienced a sense of socio-emotional discomfort (Topping, Smith, Swanson, and Elliot, 2000), they still perceived an increase in personal motivation as a result of their active participation in peer assessment (Brindley and Scoffield, 1998), including a heightened sense of engagement and concentration. Peer assessment offers students an opportunity to compare their work to that of others. Brindley and Scoffield's study (1998) supports the student view that there is more ownership of the learning experience.

While peer evaluation has the potential to provide valuable feedback to learners, it can foster a classroom environment of distrust and high competitiveness when implemented in a clumsy fashion (Levine, 2008). Students need high-quality and effective peer evaluation to feel comfortable that their teammates are contributing their fair share of the group work

NEW DIRECTIONS FOR TEACHING AND LEARNING • DOI: 10.1002/tl

(Levine, 2008). When done well, engaging students in peer assessment and feedback can be a valuable exercise in self-development (Brindley and Scoffield, 1998).

Knowing that they will receive grades or points from peer assessments is a powerful incentive for students to prepare for and participate in the group work of the course (Michaelsen, 1992). However, the peer evaluation process also may reduce student motivation to participate unless its use is clearly communicated and aligned with students' expectations and values for its use (Chen and Lou, 2004). Peer assessment is not a set prescriptive process, but rather one that may take time to develop and may also change over time depending on the course content, class size, the curriculum, the university culture, and the students themselves.

Guidelines for Implementing Peer Assessment and Evaluation

Michaelsen (1992) strongly recommended that instructors set student expectations early and consider collaboratively determining assessment dimensions such as the weight each will contribute to final grades and the frequency with which they are administered. Peer assessment and evaluation should also be aligned with grading policies, classroom procedures, and group activities (Michaelsen, Knight, and Fink, 2004), and instructors should offer resources for students on how to provide constructive evaluation and feedback.

Setting Expectations. The process of involving students early offers the opportunity to determine what dimensions and assessment criteria are relevant to the activities and course objectives of the TBL classroom. This is generally done as soon as students understand how team-based learning works, usually no later than the third class (Michaelsen, Knight, and Fink, 2004). The assessment literature provides a thorough examination of the dimensions and criteria measured by peer assessments in TBL, and forms that can be accessed via the Web site www.teambasedlearning.org/ndtl offer other examples as well. Typically criteria include group process and individual task and individual group behavior contributions such as cooperation, flexibility, dependability, attendance, attitude, respect for team members, preparedness, initiative, leadership, communication, and decision making (Dominick, Reilly, and McGourty, 1997; Schelf-hout, Dochy, and Janssens, 2004; Thackeray and Wheeler, 2006).

Involving Students in Designing Instruments and Procedures. Lane (2007) describes the advantage of allowing peer assessment instruments and procedures to be developed by engineering students as opposed to faculty, which is similar to the early team-building exercise Michaelsen used (1992, 2004) when students engage in setting their own grade weights. Michaelsen identifies three considerations for instructors who are considering how much "grade weight" (p. 113) to give to their peer assessment. First, peer evaluations should be weighted so that students take the process seriously in terms of impact on their final individual grade. Next, the instructor must be comfortable with administration of the instrument. Third, it should address student concerns for fairness and equity.

When students develop their own assessments, they become invested in the outcomes of their evaluation efforts, resulting in greater ownership for the assessment criteria and associated feedback. Put simply, students support that which they help to create. Falchikov and Goldfinch (2000) suggest that student familiarity with and ownership of assessment criteria also tend to foster peer assessment validity and recommend student involvement in their determination.

Using Periodic Formative Assessments. Using periodic formative assessments has a number of advantages. When used at the end of learning modules, they help assuage student concerns about equity issues (Gueldenzoph and May, 2002; Haberyan, 2007; Levine, 2008). In addition, using periodic formative assessments allows students the opportunity to develop their skills at giving assessments before doing a final summative evaluation (Levine, 2008). Periodic assessments also promote team effectiveness and enable students to improve their own skills. Students who are unaware that their behaviors are unacceptable to team members learn early to change behaviors that may be unproductive or disruptive to the team (Michaelsen, Knight, and Fink, 2004). Some additional suggestions for the process include providing a mechanism for giving anonymous or confidential comments, making sure that members give each other both positive and negative comments, and giving later feedback the most weight (Michaelsen, 2004). Depending on the environment, peer evaluations may be used at the midpoint and at the end of a course. Implementing too many rounds of peer evaluation, however, may have drawbacks. These include disruption to team development and validating the role of a dominant participant early in the semester (Michaelsen, Knight, and Fink, 2004).

Preparing Learners for Feedback. It is important to prepare learners before asking them to participate in peer evaluation. It should not be assumed that students understand how to perform peer evaluation or that they have been exposed to it in other course work. In demonstrating how peer assessment is done in a graduate educational psychology writing course, for example, Topping, Smith, Swanson, and Elliot (2000) reported using a demonstration of an instructor conducting a critical analysis of their own peer-reviewed journal publication to highlight areas for improvement as a means of providing a model for students to follow in conducting their own peer assessments. Students who are intellectually capable but perhaps socially unskilled can learn through exposure to feedback from their peers who have similar outcomes at stake (Michaelsen, 1992).

Giving appropriate and constructive feedback is a skill that takes time and instruction to do well. Early in the semester or on the evaluation form, a verbal or brief written explanation may be provided to students (Levine, 2008). This offers students a guide to follow, which may ease any concerns on what feedback should be gathered and how it should be structured to be most effective. It may be useful to communicate the hallmarks of effective feedback so students understand what is expected and to ease the social discomfort that may come with the process. Characteristics of effective feedback are addressed at the conclusion of this chapter.

Anonymous Versus "Owned" Assessments and Evaluations. Although there is universal agreement among TBL users that the instructor needs to know who is saying what to whom, there is considerable debate about how much students should know about the source of the scores and comments they receive from their peers. On one hand, students may be more honest when they know their peers will not know which team member offered the feedback. On the other hand, when students do not own the feedback they give (that is, the receiver does not know who gave it), they may provide harsher criticisms and evaluations (Lane, 2007) and as a result have a negative impact on the relationships between team members. If feedback is done correctly, either approach can be successful. Understanding your environment, communicating with students in the process, and being consistent in the administration of peer assessments are key. These suggestions seek to remedy student concerns about fairness, remove the mystery surrounding its contribution to the final course grade, and set expectations about the student and teacher role in the TBL environment.

Customizing the Process. Every educational environment is different, so the use of a peer evaluation instrument for one setting might not be appropriate for another institution or discipline. In many respects, peer review is best received in an environment in which there is a culture of professionalism and a minimum amount of competition and mistrust. The more courses that promote and encourage peer review, the better students will accept it and use it constructively (Levine, 2008).

Part of determining what is right for the particular environment includes determining the frequency with which the peer assessment process will be used. Brooks and Ammons (2003) found that in a cross-disciplinary course with modules on accounting, marketing, and management, implementing peer assessments every four weeks, for a total of three times during the semester, reduced the variation of rating among students. In a human learning undergraduate course, the instructor uses a formative assessment at midsemester and a summative peer evaluation at the end. Levine (2008) also advocates a similar process of two times during the semester for students in a clinical graduate course (Levine and others, 2004).

Assessment Instruments and Approaches

For instructors who lack the time or interest to design a peer assessment in its entirety, excellent instruments are available. We recommend considering five approaches. Two of the approaches were developed by Michaelsen and Fink and are described in detail in Michaelsen, Knight, and Fink (2004);

the related forms are contained there as well. Briefly, in the Michaelsen method (2002), students are expected to assign teammates a score based on the extent to which they believe their teammates contributed to the overall team performance. For example, in a six-person team, fifty points are given to each student to divide among five team members (self-excluded), with a minimum possible score of seven, average of ten, and maximum of thirteen (Levine, 2008). The overall score for an individual is then calculated by summing the scores received from each teammate. Students also have an opportunity to include qualitative comments. This method requires that students make distinctions among peer performances; not everyone can receive a ten.

In the Fink method, students are given one hundred points and prompted to divide them among team members based on their degree of contributions. All members then get a peer score that is the sum of the points they are awarded by each team members and then this total is multiplied by the their mean readiness assurance test score (or another group score) to come up with an adjusted group score. Students are also prompted to provide qualitative feedback with justification for the number of points that were assigned. This method differs from the Michaelsen method in that students may assign all one hundred points to each peer; there is no required differentiation of points.

A third approach, developed by Paul Koles for use with year-long medical student teams, is outlined in more detail in Levine (2008). It includes both a comprehensive quantitative feedback section capturing ratings on cooperative learning skills, self-directed learning, and interpersonal skills and qualitative questions. Qualitative questions probe the most valuable contributions a person makes to the team and the most important thing a person could do to more effectively help the team (Levine, 2008). Feedback is anonymous.

A fourth approach, outlined in Chapter Six in this volume, involves using qualitative data (peer comments given and received) as a "difference maker" for students whose grades fall on a borderline. Finally, Lane (2007) describes an approach that involves students in creating the instruments and procedures that they will use for collecting quantitative and qualitative peer evaluation data that is then used to provide feedback and grading input for the members of their team. (All five of these approaches and the forms that support their implementation are available online by clicking on the Peer Evaluations link at www.teambasedlearning.org/ndtl.)

Conclusion

Peer assessments and evaluations are essential components of team-based learning. Clearly the process of administering peer evaluation in higher education is a challenging endeavor, especially for instructors new to TBL. As the instructional guidelines and student concerns demonstrate, there is much to consider. As a review of the methods here indicates, there is no single best way to conduct peer evaluation; each method brings with it advantages and potential problems. Nevertheless, there are some basic principles to keep in mind when establishing a TBL program with a peer evaluation component:

- The skill of performing evaluation is not intuitive. It is useful to assume that most learners have never been taught how to give feedback. Brief written or verbal instruction on how to provide constructive evaluation may prove extremely helpful in allaying students' fears about the process of giving (and receiving) peer review. At a minimum, students should understand the seven characteristics of providing helpful feedback to peers. These characteristics include providing feedback that is descriptive rather than evaluative; being specific, honest and sincere, relevant, timely, in context, desired by the receiver, and concerned with behavior one has the control to change (Michaelsen and Schultheiss, 1988).
- As with any other skill, practice is essential in order to become comfortable with the process. Students need to be able to practice peer review in a safe environment before they can easily apply it for a grade. In most teaching situations, this can be accomplished through a midcourse peer review.
- In many respects, peer review is best received in an environment in which there is a culture of professionalism and a minimal amount of competition and mistrust. The more that courses promote and encourage peer review, the better students will accept it and use it constructively.
- With quantitative evaluations, if students are not forced to discriminate among their teammates, such as giving out only a set number of points, the scores are likely to be highly inflated.
- Students are more comfortable giving qualitative feedback than quantitative feedback. As a result, this might be the easier feedback to begin with for the educator who is reluctant to force a discriminatory quantitative evaluation on the students. However, unless peer evaluations have teeth, groups are vulnerable to students who are prone to social loafing.

Although the process of establishing a peer evaluation system can be frustrating (no one ever got a teaching award for putting together a good peer evaluation), ultimately it is an essential tool for reinforcing the individual accountability so vital to the TBL. Many students need peer review to offset their fear that they will be burdened by having to carry their group. We recommend experimenting with a variety of methods until you find one that works for you in your particular environment. One bit of good news is that if students are accustomed to peer evaluation at an early point in their college careers, the skills will likely transfer across collaborative partnerships in other educational and professional settings (Brooks and Ammons, 2003).

References

Boud, D., Cohen, R., and Sampson, J. "Peer Learning and Assessment." *Assessment and Evaluation in Higher Education*, 1999, 24(4), 413–426.

Brindley, C., and Scoffield, S. "Peer Assessment in Undergraduate Programs." *Teaching in Higher Education,* 1998, *3*(1), 79–89.

Brooks, C. M., and Ammons, J. L. "Free Riding in Group Projects and the Effects of Timing, Frequency, and Specificity of Criteria in Peer Assessments." *Journal of Education for Business,* 2003, *78*(5), 268–272.

Chen, Y., and Lou, H. "Students' Perceptions of Peer Evaluation: Expectancy Perspective." *Journal of Education for Business,* 2004, *79*(5), 275–282.

Cheng, W., and Warren, M. "Making a Difference: Using Peers to Assess Individual Students' contributions to a Group Project." *Teaching in Higher Education,* 2000, *5*(2), 243–255.

Dochy, F., Segers, M., and Sluijsmans, D. "The Use of Self, Peer, and Co-Assessment in Higher Education: A Review." *Studies in Higher Education,* 1999, *24*(3), 331–350.

Dominick, P. G., Reilly, R. R., and McGourty, J. W. "The Effects of Peer Feedback on Team Member Behavior." *Group and Organization Management,* 1997, *22*(4), 508–519.

Falchikov, N., and Goldfinch, J. "Student Peer Assessment in Higher Education: A Meta-Analysis Comparing Peer and Teacher Marks." *Review of Educational Research,* 2000, *70*(3), 287–322.

Gatfield, T. "Examining Student Satisfaction with Group Projects and Peer Assessment." *Assessment and Evaluation in Higher Education,* 1999, *24*(4), 365–377.

Gueldenzoph, L. E., and May, G. L. "Collaborative Peer Evaluation: Best Practices for Group Member Assessments." *Business Communication Quarterly,* 2002, *65*(1), 9–20.

Haberyan, A. "Team-Based Learning in an Industrial/Organizational Psychology Course." *North American Journal of Psychology,* 2007, *9*(1), 143–152.

Lane, D. "Engineering Feedback: A Student-Developed Approach to the Assessment of Peer Evaluation in Civil Engineering." Chicago: National Communication Association, 2007.

Levine, R. E. "Peer Assessment in Team-Based Learning." In L. K. Michaelsen, D. X. Parmalee, K. K. McMahon, and R. E. Levine (eds.), *Team-Based Learning for Health Professions Education.* Sterling, Va.: Stylus, 2008.

Levine, R. E., O'Boyle, M., Haidet, P., Lynn, D. J., Stone, M. M., Wolf, D. V., and Paniagua, F. A. "Transforming a Clinical Clerkship with Team Learning." *Teaching and Learning in Medicine,* 2004, *16*(3), 270–275.

Michaelsen, L. K. "Team Learning: A Comprehensive Approach for Harnessing the Power of Small Groups in Higher Education." *To Improve the Academy,* 1992, *11,* 107–122.

Michaelsen, L. K., Knight, A. B., and Fink, D. L. *Team-Based Learning: A Transformative Use of Small Groups.* Westport, Conn.: Praeger, 2004.

Michaelsen, L. K., and Schultheiss, E. E. "Making Feedback Helpful." *Organizational Behavior Teaching Review,* 1988, *13*(1), 109–113.

Paswan, A. K., and Gollakota, K. "Dimensions of Peer Evaluation, Overall Satisfaction, and Overall Evaluation: An Investigation in a Group Task Environment." *Journal of Education for Business,* 2004, *79*(4), 275–231.

Schelfhout, W., Dochy, F., and Janssens, S. "The Use of Self, Peer, and Teacher Assessment as a Feedback System in a Learning Environment Aimed at Fostering Skills of Cooperation in an Entrepreneurial Context." *Assessment and Evaluation in Higher Education,* 2004, *29*(2), 177–201.

Searby, M., and Ewers, T. "An Evaluation of the Use of Peer Assessment in Higher Education: A Case Study in the School of Music, Kingston University." *Assessment and Evaluation in Higher Education,* 1997, *22*(4), 371–383.

Thackeray, R., and Wheeler, M. L. "Innovations in Social Marketing Education: A Team-Based Learning Approach." *Social Marketing Quarterly,* 2006, *12*(3), 42–48.

Topping, K. "Trends in Peer Learning." *Educational Psychology,* 2005, *25*(6), 631–645.

Topping, K. J., Smith, E. F., Swanson, I., and Elliot, A. "Formative Peer Assessment of Academic Writing between Postgraduate Students." *Assessment & Evaluation in Higher Education,* 2000, *25*(2), 149–170.

CHRISTINA M. CESTONE *is from the Department of Educational Psychology at The University of Texas at Austin.*

RUTH E. LEVINE *is the Clarence Ross Miller Professor of Psychiatry and Internal Medicine in the Department of Psychiatry and Behavioral Sciences at The University of Texas Medical Branch, Galveston.*

DEREK R. LANE *is an associate dean in the College of Communications and Information Studies and associate professor in the Department of Communication at the University of Kentucky*

NEW DIRECTIONS FOR TEACHING AND LEARNING • DOI: 10.1002/tl

The purpose of instructional technology is to make things possible that are otherwise not, or to make easier things that otherwise are difficult. This chapter describes a few of the tweaks to team-based learning that the authors have developed using technology.

Technological Alternatives to Paper-Based Components of Team-Based Learning

Daniel H. Robinson, Joshua D. Walker

We have been using components of team-based learning (TBL) in two undergraduate courses at the University of Texas for several years: an educational psychology survey course—Cognition, Human Learning and Motivation—and Introduction to Statistics. In this chapter, we describe how we used technology in classes of fifty to seventy students to improve the implementation of three key TBL activities: readiness assurance tests, reporting complex team assignments, and providing feedback on peer evaluations.

Readiness Assurance Tests

For a number of years, we used the individual-plus-team-testing sequence for the readiness assurance process (RAP), including the immediate feedback assessment technique (IF-AT) forms, and experienced a number of positive learning and team development outcomes along the lines of those described elsewhere in this volume. However, we also encountered several problems that led us to consider a technology-based alternative to paper tests and IF-ATs.

Problems with Paper Tests and IF-ATs. We encountered problems with paper tests and IF-ATs in four areas: logistics, the potential for cheating, test security, and problems with the forms themselves. Even with team

folders (see Michaelsen, Knight, and Fink, 2004), ensuring that each student receives and returns a copy of the test and answer sheet becomes difficult as class size increases. This task is complicated for instructors who use alternate forms of the test form to discourage cheating. Even if they require students to write their names on the test forms themselves (as well as their answer sheets) and penalize students who fail to turn them in before leaving, students occasionally forget and leave the room without turning them in. This compromises item and test security because—if and when instructors do get the test form back from the student—they have no way of knowing whether the student copied the items for later use by friends. Finally, the IF-AT forms themselves also have disadvantages, including cost (a minimum order is just over a hundred dollars) and susceptibility to cheating (students can see the stars with a high-powered penlight laser). We also had a batch of forms on which the covering had dried out so that students could not scratch it off without scratching off the star as well.

Our Computer-Based Alternative. A few years ago, we began to develop an online team-based testing (TBT) system that would incorporate all of the desirable features of the IF-AT while avoiding some of the pitfalls. (For a lengthier description of our system, see Robinson, Sweet, and Mayrath, 2008.) At the heart of TBL is engaged dialogue, so we wanted students to be able to sit close to each other and see each other's body language and facial expressions—which would be almost impossible in a typical computer lab in which computers are placed side-by-side in rows and columns. Fortunately, at the University of Texas, by using a combination of student- and university-owned laptops, we can provide each student with a computer and space for fifty to seventy students to use them.

On the days we give readiness assurance tests (RATs), we allow students to arrive at class a few minutes early to log in to the system. As with paper-based tests, students who arrive late are still expected to finish within the allotted time. Once students log into the TBT system, they answer multiple-choice questions on their computer. Early on, we presented the questions randomly ordered and one at a time, and with randomly ordered answer alternatives, as a means of discouraging cheating. However, some students were adamantly opposed to the one-question-at-a-time option because they wanted to be able to go back and change their answers if they wished, although there is no evidence that this improves test performance (Bodmann and Robinson, 2005). Thus, on the individual readiness assurance test (iRAT), we still present the questions and answer alternatives in random order to discourage cheating, but we now allow students to scroll to see all the questions. They click to make their selections and then click a submit button when finished.

Once all of the team members have submitted their iRAT, the team readiness assurance test (tRAT) becomes available on the following screen (a password is required), and a designated team member submits answers for the team and relays feedback on their choices. The remaining members log in to an area where the order of the questions is the same for everyone and they can see their own iRAT answers.

Beyond the security of randomly ordered questions for individual tests and the convenience of uniformly reordered questions for team tests, we soon discovered another advantage of the electronic format. With paper-based testing, when all students had the same form with the same order of multiple-choice options, we had noticed that they could simply refer to the answer options by letter when counting votes to reach consensus on team answers (for example, "I put A," "I put B"). Students typically began by going around the circle reporting the letter of the answer they chose and would move forward based on a majority vote. After watching team interactions that occur with TBT, we are convinced that having the opportunity to decide on a team answer by simply stating the letters related to the answer options sometimes short-circuits the more meaningful consensus-seeking dialogues intended by collaborative learning environments and can result in more incorrect answers. So in TBT, the response options on the iRATs are randomly ordered and there are no response labels such as letters or numbers. This forces students to read the answer alternatives aloud (because they cannot vote simply by referring to the letters that represent the options) and increases the likelihood of thinking more carefully about the course vocabulary and discussing more deeply before rendering their decisions. In fact, we are in the process of analyzing data that reveals decisions take longer with TBT and result in higher tRAT scores (Robinson, 2008).

Similar to the IF-AT forms, teams are required to keep trying until they answer correctly. Each time a team answers incorrectly, 50 percent of the points for that item are removed. Thus, for a five-option question, item points can range from 100 percent to about 6 percent: after the first wrong choice, the most they can get for that item is 50 percent of the point value; after the second wrong choice, the most they can get is 25 percent; and so on. As a result, TBT maintains the immediate feedback and partial credit advantages of the IF-AT.

Once teams submit their final answer, they automatically receive their score for that question. Again similar to the IF-AT, throughout the team testing process, correct answers are revealed and individuals are able to score their own test. If a team wants to appeal a question, they write it out by hand on paper and submit it to the instructor by the end of class. Immediately after class, we take the appeals to the office and rule on them right away. Results of team scores and bonus points are announced by posting on the classroom management system within a few hours of the test. For teams that receive the highest score, each team member receives three bonus points added to the individual test score. Second-place teams receive two points, and third-place teams receive one point. Of course, there are ties so frequently at least half the teams receive bonus points. We also typically award at least one appeal for each test, so teams are encouraged to seriously consider the accuracy of each item. Our experience with the testing process is that we witness students digging into the material more deeply than any other testing sequence we have seen. We encourage anyone who is interested in using TBT to contact us because the software is open source and free to the public.

Reporting Complex Team Assignments

Perhaps the most challenging component of TBL for us has been developing good team activities. At the same time, this has been the most rewarding component because it forces us to consider ways in which students should be able to enrich their understanding of the course content. For the course we teach on cognition, human learning, and motivation, we decided to focus on the studying and learning strategies that are a major part of the course. We have students do assignments over two chapters at a time, with six assignments for the course. These assignments are designed to capitalize on the TBL principles to enhance learning and performance.

As with any other TBL component, we believe that both individual and team accountability are required to optimize learning. As part of the curriculum, we stress that information found in textbooks can be represented in many ways and that an optimal form of representation is one that allows us to see what we might not have seen otherwise (Tukey, 1977). For example, a row-and-column graphic organizer may reveal comparison relations that are obscured in other displays. Thus, students are aware that outlines and lists are not the only forms of note taking. Preferably, they will create more graphical forms of notes that use space to demonstrate relations and allow visual discoveries. Our goal for these assignments is to have students represent course content in ways that lead to optimal and efficient learning. We accomplish this through an assignment that requires them to consider the features of information that make it difficult for learners to understand and the features of information that enable us to use that information in the future. Thus, in the spirit of TBL, we wanted to allow differences in choices about how to represent the content but also a way to meld individual work into a team product that could be shared with the class as a whole and would stimulate discussion and debate—all within a seventy-five-minute class period.

To save class time, we require students to read two chapters from the textbook and develop an individual PowerPoint file that contains four sets of notes over what section of each chapter contains the content they think is most important (relevant, useful, or something else) and the most difficult to learn. They must also upload their PowerPoint in their team's course management file exchange by midnight before the 11:00 A.M. class.

As the instructors, we create teams and also an entire class team or group in the course management system. Students then go to Communication: Group Pages; they select their team and then File Exchange. This gives

NEW DIRECTIONS FOR TEACHING AND LEARNING • DOI: 10.1002/tl

their teammates a chance to look at everyone's work before arriving at class. We use PowerPoint because it has drawing tools that allow students to enhance and enrich their concept notes by creating a wide variety of display typefaces and including pictures that support their conclusions.

We use the first thirty minutes of class for teams to decide whose notes to share with the class and create a team PowerPoint file by copying, pasting, and editing from members' individual work. This activity is fun to observe as students bring considerable energy to the task of discussing the rationales of members' individual decisions. Although there are no absolute right and wrong selections, teams are aware that the entire class will critique their choices, and we consider these critiques in assigning grades. Then, using a computer and projector, we go to the entire class group page and view the teams' assignments by projecting the slide shows on the screen. This is similar to the "gallery walk" some TBL instructors use (see Sweet, Michaelsen, and Wright, 2007).

We score each of the group slide shows for accuracy and originality. Total assignment scores for individuals consist of three parts. First is their individual contribution, which we can access by downloading their Power-Point file from the course management system. Students receive the most points if they post their file by midnight the night before and if it appears they contributed something that required effort. Second is whether they showed up for class that day. Third, each member receives their team's score on the slide show they created and presented. In addition, students use the information about their teammates' contributions in their later judgments for peer evaluations.

We have found that the teams are very interested in viewing the other teams' work. In addition, we consistently have received positive feedback from the students regarding the assignments; they frequently report that they view the team slides in preparation for the tests, which are generally given the following class period.

Providing Feedback on Peer Evaluations

The third adjustment we have made involving computers is related to the way in which we obtain and share feedback within teams. When we began implementing TBL, we struggled with how to incorporate peer evaluations in our grading system. After trying several ways to do peer evaluations, we settled on having students complete a simple teammate feedback form at least two, and more often three, times during the semester. The form asks them to provide a short answer to the following two questions for each member of their team: "Something I appreciate about this person is . . ." and "Something I would like to request of this person is . . ."

Both we and the students like the outcomes of the feedback process; however, we found ourselves almost buried in paperwork. We would collect fifty to seventy hand-written forms. Then we would have to type requests and appreciations for each student from their teammates and then print and distribute them as quickly as possible. Even with two of us working to turn the feedback around, it was always more than a week before the students learned what their teammates thought about their contributions to the team.

Technology to the Rescue. Our interim solution to the problem is that we use e-mail to collect the peer input and distribute the results. We simply e-mail the teammate feedback forms and their teammates' names to the students and ask they reply. We copy and paste the responses into a large word processing file for our own records and individual files that we e-mail back to the students, with the identifying information omitted. The electronic copying and pasting and then e-mailing saves valuable time over the paper-based system and allows us to deliver the feedback to the students more quickly.

Our long-term solution that our programmers are finishing is a Web-based system where students can log in and enter the feedback. The program will then sort the feedback and allow students to log in and view the results. This system, when completed, will also be open source and free to the public. It is very easy to use, and we encourage you to contact us if you are interested in using it.

Translating Comments into Grades. One of the unique features of the teammate feedback process is that even though we do not collect any quantitative data, the peer comments can, and in some cases do, raise students' final letter grade. We tell students that for the most part, the comments will not be used or even read by the instructor. However, at the end of the course, a few students fall just short of a grade cutoff and come in to ask us if they can do anything to raise the grade. We tell students that, if they face this situation, then their peers' comments will become the deciding factor. If the comments are mostly positive or if they started a bit rough early in the semester but clearly improved over the course, then we give them the few points. If the comments are negative, that shows us how committed the student was to the course and the answer is no.

Furthermore, as a result of discussions during the preparation of this chapter, we plan to tweak the way we use teammate feedback in a way that we are confident will increase its already positive impact. In future classes, we will give students a short article to read, "Making Feedback Helpful" (Michaelsen and Schulteiss, 1988), and tell them that in borderline cases, "First, we will look at the evaluations you *gave* and if it looks like you were serious about trying to give helpful feedback, then we'll look at the feedback you *received* from your peers and, based on the two, we'll decide about raising your grade." Because students never know whether they will be close to a grade cutoff, the teammate feedback process used in that way will provide a grade-based incentive for learning how to give helpful feedback, using that knowledge to provide feedback to members of their team, and being a responsible team member.

Conclusion

We are fans of TBL and will continue to use many of its features in our courses. We do not believe that technology is the answer to every educational problem. We also realize that often educators rush to implement technology unnecessarily, and it sometimes has negative outcomes. Our goal in using technology has been to avoid negative outcomes and simply improve an already great system—one that after using, we could not go back to our previous instructional methods and still enjoy teaching.

References

Bodmann, S. M., and Robinson, D. H. "Speed and Performance Differences Among Computer-Based and Paper-Pencil Tests." *Journal of Educational Computing Research,* 2004, *31,* 51–60.

Michaelsen, L. K., Knight, A. B., and Fink, L. D. (eds.) *Team-Based Learning: A Transformative Use of Small Groups in College Teaching.* Sterling, Va.: Stylus, 2004.

Michaelsen, L. K., and Schultheiss, E. E. "Making Feedback Helpful." *Organizational Behavior Teaching Review,* 1988, *13*(1), 109–113.

Robinson, D. H. "Using Alternate Test Forms in Team-Based Testing to Prolong and Enhance Team Deliberations." Manuscript in preparation, 2008.

Robinson, D. H., Sweet, M. S., and Mayrath, M. "Computer-Based Team-Based Testing." In D. H. Robinson and G. Schraw (eds.), *Current Perspectives on Cognition, Learning, and Instruction: Recent Innovations in Educational Technology That Facilitate Student Learning.* Charlotte, NC: Information Age, 2008.

Sweet, M. M., Michaelsen, L. K., and Wright, C. "Simultaneous Report: A Reliable Method to Stimulate Class Discussion." *Decision Sciences Journal of Innovative Education,* 2008, *6*(2).

Tukey, J. W. *Exploratory Data Analysis.* Reading, Mass.: Addison-Wesley, 1977.

DANIEL H. ROBINSON *is an associate professor of educational psychology at the University of Texas at Austin.*

JOSHUA D. WALKER *is a graduate student in educational psychology at the University of Texas at Austin.*

In implementing team-based learning in a purely online, asynchronous course, the authors advise planning early and planning well, a process for which they provide specific advice.

Team-Based Learning in Asynchronous Online Settings

Sunay Palsolé, Carolyn Awalt

Team-based learning (TBL) has been shown to improve student learning in a variety of settings (Michaelsen, Knight, and Fink, 2004). In a majority of cases, team-based learning (TBL) has been implemented in face-to-face formats and occasionally in blended learning formats, which are partially online partially and face-to-face in a classroom (Freeman, 2004). The Sloan Consortium surveys (Allen and Seaman, 2007) report a steady increase in the enrollments in online courses, and this is borne out by data gathered at the University of Texas at El Paso. Over the past five years, we have faced an increase in the demand for courses in flexible learning formats (blended and 100 percent online), with enrollment increasing by an average of 20 percent each year. With the unequivocal efficacy of TBL in the traditional face-to-face class format, it became imperative to find a way to implement it in flexible learning format courses. This chapter describes the implementation of asynchronous TBL in a fully online course and provides some practical strategies for practitioners interested in such implementations.

Keeping the four basic principles of TBL in mind (see Chapter One) during the design process, we first implemented TBL strategies in a fully online course in fall 2005 using a combination of testing and synchronous chat tools. Table 7.1 gives the equivalencies in the online environment of processes that are usually followed in a face-to-face environment.

The course that we redesigned for online delivery using TBL was a large undergraduate course with an enrollment of approximately about 110 students. Although this new teaching strategy seemed to work after students

NEW DIRECTIONS FOR TEACHING AND LEARNING, no. 116, Winter 2008 © Wiley Periodicals, Inc.
Published online in Wiley InterScience (www.interscience.wiley.com) • DOI: 10.1002/tl.336

Table 7.1. Equivalencies of Face-to-Face to Online Class Activities

Traditional Face-to-Face Class	Online Class
Preclass preparation (usually assigned textbook readings)	Assigned readings from books, Web sites, discovery questions, and so forth.
Multiple-choice individual readiness assurance tests (iRat) using Scantrons	Multiple-choice iRAT using online testing tools.
Team readiness assurance tests (tRAT) with immediate feedback assessment technique forms	tRAT based a discussion board over two days. Team leader (assigned in advance on a rotating basis) compiles answers and submits team answers. Team reporter compiles discussion and posts gist of the discussion to the common board. Feedback on RAT.
Mini lecture based on RAT results.	Mini lecture based on RAT results and discussion is added to the week's lecture.
Five to seven RATs per course— to prepare for application activities; may be followed by a peer evaluation	Five RATs in weeks 3, 6, 9, 12, and 15. Schedule matches the stages of the team project, which is due at the end of the semester. Peer evaluations are done after each RAT on an Excel spreadsheet that each individual uploads as an assignment.
Grading of team application activities typically done by instructor and may include evaluations from other teams; individual scores may be modified base on a postactivity peer evaluation. 20 percent = peer evaluation.	Team projects are graded as follows: 50 percent = individual grade (by instructor's assessment of contribution on assignment using a rubric that was created by team); 30 percent = team grade;
Often includes an end-of-semester reflective assignment.	End of semester is wrapped up with a reflective assignment.

became accustomed to the timetables, we had increasing complaints from students about finding convenient times required to work synchronously for taking the individual and team readiness assurance tests (respectively, iRATs and tRATs). Given the fact that most students tend to take fully online courses for the time and space flexibility afforded to them, it became necessary to find a solution to doing TBL in asynchronous modalities.

A revised version of asynchronous TBL was implemented in fall 2006 with a follow-up in fall 2007. The 2006 course, Interdisciplinary Technology and Society, had an enrollment of seventy-four students. We decided to leverage the capability of instant feedback by using the built-in test tools in our learning management system and the fact that we could elicit thoughtful responses (Markel, 2001; Freeman, 2004, Palloff and Pratt, 2005) from the students using the discussion board tool. We also took into account that time expands in online discussions (Meyer, 2003) and designed the learning process to account for this.

Our first design revisions were focused on modifying our procedures to promote team cohesion better. Then, before we launched the actual course, we refined the procedures based on feedback from four run-throughs with student workers playing the part of students.

Setup

One of the most important things to keep in mind when teaching online courses is that you cannot expect students to be able to find matching times for synchronous work, and this is particularly true when they are taking online courses that are designed specifically to afford them time and space flexibility. Nevertheless, tasks can be designed to achieve the desired student engagement provided that extra time is incorporated to enable team interactions to occur.

To allow students extra time, we required learning teams to post to the discussion board every week and provide thoughtful feedback to every member of the team. This established the expectation on the part of the students that discussion was an important part of the class. We then set up teams to participate in TBL exercises. We explained to the students why TBL was important and the exact procedures that would be followed.

Creating Teams. We chose to create five-member teams using the automated tool in our learning management system. Three semesters of study convinced us that automated team selection created team assignments that were just as diverse as, and sometimes more diverse than, those created by manual processes used by the instructor and saved time overall. Teams were permanent and were not allowed to change. We asked teams to create their own team contracts and establish their strategy for working together. To have teams discover their team assets, we had them post introductions of themselves with their strengths and weaknesses and their overall goals for the class in their team discussion board, which is somewhat similar to Salmon's five-stage framework (2003). Borrowing from Harasim, Hiltz, Teles, and Turoff (1995) the idea that students working in a virtual environment need to discover common goals and objectives to be successful, we then asked the team members to look at each other's strengths and weaknesses and outline what they would do to build a support structure. We asked each team to write this up as a formal support document and post it in their team files area in WebCT.

Creating Accountability. We created multiple-choice tests using the learning management system's built-in test and assessment tools. Multiple-choice tests were duplicated so they could be used by the individual students to ensure accountability for individual preparation and for the tRAT after the team's discussion in its discussion board. Each team activity was followed by a peer evaluation carried out using a spreadsheet provided to the team or a tool built at the University of Texas at El Paso specifically for that purpose and uploaded by each team as an assignment. In the case of the spreadsheet, grades were tallied using macros.

Promoting Team Learning and Development. Our previous experience and research demonstrates that engaging learners in the online collaborative environment requires that all teams (and members) must feel that their ideas are being heard and discussed (McConnell, 2006). To generate this engagement and to promote team development, we created a system of sharing and voting for the best team projects. Team products were shared in a discussion or drop box area, and every member of the class voted on the best product (they could not vote for their own team) and provided feedback. The results were tallied, and the winning team was awarded extra points that amounted to about 5 percent of the final project grade. This is done so there is enough incentive for teams to do well, but not so much as to bring in the factor of greed. We also added a reflection assignment that teams turned in every four weeks. For this assignment, they examined their goals set at the beginning of the class and evaluated whether they were on target. We spent significant time writing questions that were indirect and open-ended queries. For example, we asked them to think about the philosophy of technology use on the El Paso-Juarez border instead of asking them to list what technologies were being used on the El Paso–Juarez border area.

Providing Frequent and Immediate Feedback. The automation of the test tool in the learning management system helped provide feedback fairly instantaneously when team leaders entered the team answers on the tRAT. Due to the nature of online work, team leaders rotated each session and were responsible for taking the tRAT based on the discussions of the assigned questions in the team discussion board. Although the teams were not present in the same space at the same time, the students' excitement in wanting to know their performance was demonstrated by the fact that most of the students checked the group grades within twenty-four hours of the team leader's submitting the team answers. We also wrote learning management system rules to allow the release of scores for the iRATs only after the team leaders had completed the tRAT. We provided feedback on the team discussion boards following completion of the tRAT. We used the discussion boards to suggest topics for our mini lectures that were created and added to the course content as a result of the students' performance on the RATs. An overview of our adaptation of the RAT to online environment appears in Figure 7.1.

How We Implemented the 4 S's. The final project was a team project and required students to look at the City of El Paso and work out changes that may need to be done (within reason) to build a sustainable ecology. We had students and teams complete five application assignments and tried to keep the 4 S's of effective team assignments in doing so: significant to students, same problem, specific choice, and simultaneous report (see Chapter One and the volume appendix). Furthermore, each assignment was designed to build up the knowledge needed to complete the final project.

Figure 7.1. The Readiness Assurance Process

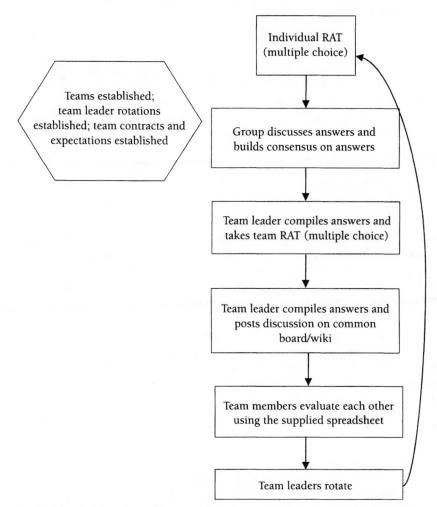

Note: Completion of the individual and team RATs takes about three to four days from start to finish.
Source: Michaelsen, Michaelson, and Black (1994). Adapted to the Online Course Environment.

Assignments were made available to all the teams at the same time on a common discussion board. An example assignment follows (*significant to students*):

> What types of renewable and alternative energy technologies will promote economic growth for a sustainable environment for the 21st century? Isolate some of the issues, support your arguments with specific references, and outline some possible solutions. Use the evaluation framework you developed in the previous assignment to help guide your solution path.

Each team had the same assignment (*same problem*) and the same time frame to turn in their work:

Day 1	Assignment is posted to a common discussion board.
Days 1–5	Team discussion, consensus building, and development of final product on Team Wiki.
Day 6	Team assignment submitted to the grading tool and posted to its discussion board. Teaching team collects discussions and posts them to the common discussion board for all teams to see (*simultaneous reporting*).
Days 6–7	Team members fill out peer evaluation forms using the spreadsheet or online tool.

We did not implement the 4 S of specific choice, since we did not think we could do this effectively. In the process of writing this chapter and discussions about the process, however, we have realized that we can implement specific choice by presenting the teams with a list of technologies and then having them choose one or a combination from the presented list. This process will be implemented in spring 2009.

We found that even when we did not have synchronous or face-to-face simultaneous reporting, the students were still excited to see what their grades were and the solutions that the other teams had produced. This was indicated by their checking their individual and team grades and seeing what other teams had come up with and posting comments about the work that the other teams had produced.

Outcomes

We measured our outcomes by looking at the overall student performance, retention rates, and student satisfaction with TBL. The results are discussed following.

Student Performance. Overall, the students performed well in our online team-based learning class. The exception was two teams that had below-average performances. We could predict the success rates of the teams by tracking the number of posts they had in the team discussion boards and also how engaged each of the team members was in looking at the products of the other teams.

Student Retention. One of the main issues commonly seen in online courses is that they face a higher rate of student attrition as compared to a traditional classroom. In both courses that implemented TBL, we realized about a 90 percent retention rate. We feel that this was achieved by helping the students set goals and reflect on them throughout the semester and the fact that being part of a functioning team helped build the right support structure to help them stay on track even if they fell a little behind at times.

Student Comments on TBL. Students were also asked to engage in a reflective exercise that asked them to think about what they had achieved in the class through teamwork and how each step contributed to their success. We also surveyed the students at the end of the semester about class effectiveness. Among their comments were these:

"It was a pain to keep doing the evaluations but I think it helped because no one could hide so everyone had to do the work."

"I had never thought that teams would work well online. I think it was interesting to do the weekly postings and exchange views."

"I won't say that I enjoyed the team learning, but this was the best experience I had working in teams."

"It was a good experience. I liked reading other teams' work and the competition. I just wish we had done better."

An overall evaluation of the class did not show any significant differences in grades compared to the face-to-face strategy, but there was significant satisfaction with teamwork when students were asked to compare their experiences in other classes where they worked in formal or informal teams.

Conclusion

Given the overall performance, experience, and feedback from the students, we feel that our adaptation of TBL in the online course was a success. Some factors that we believe contributed to the success are an early team-building exercise that helped the teams identify strengths and weaknesses and build a support structure and frequent peer evaluations that helped keep the teams on track. This was very important since the teams did not have a chance to meet, so receiving frequent feedback on their individual contributions to the team did contribute to team success. In addition, the team competition helped create interteam excitement for the best finished product, and the fact that the best-performing team was selected by its peers was a great contributing factor in the success of the teams.

The team assignments were designed to cascade into each other and used products from previous assignments for the next assignment. This sequencing was a little difficult to do, but it was valuable to help the teams see the pathway to the big picture final product.

Overall we realized that the teams needed a lot of training in the beginning about Netiquette if they were to succeed well without misinterpreting responses given to queries. Moreover, it became apparent that while most aspects of classical TBL can be implemented in online formats, the procedures for the readiness assurance process and application exercises have to be modified to fit the online environment.

Finally, applying the TBL strategy in an online environment was a time-consuming task to develop and implement the first time, but the overall results of the student satisfaction surveys made it a worthwhile and success-ful enterprise.

Next Steps

Student feedback indicated that they valued their experiences with team build-ing in the online courses. They also indicated that the spreadsheet evaluation tool was preferable to the online tool (which was easier to use) because it let them evaluate each other on much broader criteria. We plan to examine newer tools that have been developed for online peer evaluations and the readiness assurance processes to see if they can be used to simplify these processes.

We have these tips for adoption:

- Plan early and plan well. Map out the entire course flow using software or a whiteboard. We found this to be valuable as we built each of the assignments and worked out submission dates and times to create as seamless a process as possible.
- Design for a few weeks, and have the material tested by students or col-leagues to iron out any wrinkles in directions or plans.
- Work out a calendar, and have a third party double-check it.
- Provide as many details as possible. If there is a misinterpretation to be made, it will be made in the online environment.
- Create flowcharts for the process, and post them in the syllabus. They help students keep track of the processes.
- Provide another assignment checklist outside the syllabus or schedule, and post reminders online.
- Conduct an early team-building exercise that has low stakes and helps teammates get to know each other.
- Be prepared in the first two weeks to answer endless queries about the work details in the class. Post a frequently asked questions list in the course.
- Set up a help board in the discussion area for the class, and encourage stu-dents to post queries to the help board first, before e-mailing you, so you can reply once and point other students to the same area.
- Encourage students to help their peers, and provide some incentive to do so.
- Be prepared to modify plans as needed. We found this to be particularly true when assigning peer evaluations. We modified the number of evalu-ations when circumstances dictated.
- Add a reflection paper toward the end of the semester to help bring all the work done in the class using TBL back into focus.

References

Allen, E., and Seaman, J. *Online Nation: Five Years of Growth in Online Learning.* Need-ham, Mass.: Sloan Consortium, 2007. Retrieved June 2, 2008, from http://www.sloan-c.org/publications/survey/index.asp.

Freeman, M. "Team-Based Learning in a Course Combining In-Class and Online Inter-action." In L. K. Michaelsen, A. B. Knight, and L. D. Fink (eds.), *Team-Based Learning: A Transformative Use of Small Groups*. Sterling, Va.: Stylus, 2004.

Harasim, L., Hiltz, S. R., Teles, L., and Turoff, M. *Learning Networks: A Field Guide to Teaching and Learning Online*. Cambridge, Mass.: MIT Press, 1995.

Markel, S. "Technology and Education Online Discussion Forums: It's in the Response." *Online Journal of Distance Learning Administration*, Summer 2001, 4(2). Retrieved June 2, 2008, from http://www.westga.edu/%7Edistance/ojdla/browsearticles.php.

McConnell, D. *E-Learning Groups and Communities*. Bristol, Pa.: Open University Press, 2006.

Meyer, K. A. "Face-to-Face Versus Threaded Discussions: The Role of Time and Higher-Order Thinking." *Journal of Asynchronous Learning Networks*, 2003, 7(3), 55–65.

Michaelsen, L. K. "Getting Started with Team-Based Learning." Retrieved June 1, 2008, from http://www.ou.edu/pii/teamlearning/docs/Getting%20Started%20with%20TBL.pdf.

Michaelsen, L. K., and Black, R. H. "Building Learning Teams: The Key to Harnessing the Power of Small Groups in Higher Education." In S. Kadel and J. Keehner (eds.), *Collaborative Learning: A Sourcebook for Higher Education*. State College, Pa.: National Center for Teaching, Learning and Assessment, 1994.

Michaelsen, L. K., Knight, A. B., and Fink, L. D. *Team-Based Learning: A Transformative Use of Small Groups*. Sterling, Va.: Stylus, 2004.

Palloff, R. M., and Pratt, K. *Lessons from the Cyberspace Classroom: The Realities of Online Teaching*. San Francisco: Jossey-Bass. 2001.

Salmon, G. *Etivities: The Key to Active Online Learning*. London: Kogan Page, 2003.

SUNAY PALSOLÉ *is the director of instructional support at the University of Texas at El Paso.*

CAROLYN AWALT *is an assistant professor in the college of education and the advisor for the Online Alternative Teachers Certificate Program.*

NEW DIRECTIONS FOR TEACHING AND LEARNING • DOI: 10.1002/tl

Appendix: Key Teaching Activities for Team-Based Learning

Teachers who do each of the following seven activities will be effective using team-based learning.

Beginning of the Course

Activity 1: Form the groups
- Ideal size: Five to seven members
- Once formed, groups are permanent for the rest of the course.
- Form the groups in a public and visible way.
    Do this in a way that distributes students' subject-relevant knowledge and experiences.
    Do not use students' grade point average.

Activity 2: Get students comfortable talking to each other and the teacher
- In the first class session, have some activities that engage students in talking to each other and to the teacher. They need to know from the beginning that this is the way this course will operate and to get comfortable doing so.

Activity 3: Set up the grading system
- The grading system should have three components:
    A set of individually graded tasks
    A set of group-graded tasks
    Peer evaluation: A way for each group to evaluate the performance of each individual in the group, and for this assessment to be factored into the course grade for each student.
- The relative weight for each of these three components (or their subcomponents) can be determined by the teacher or the class. The grade-weight-setting exercise (described in Appendix B of Michaelsen, Knight, and Fink, 2004) is an effective way for the class to do this.
- Graded group work can vary in its relative weight, but the quality of the group work needs to matter. Therefore, this portion of the total course grade should be worth at least 20 to 40 percent of the total course grade.

During the Course

Activity 4: Use application exercises that are good for groups
- Application exercises can be graded or ungraded. Either way, however, it is essential that the groups learn how good their answers were (or were not).

- Construct these exercises so that:
  The tasks are meaningful and related to the ultimate learning goals.
  Successful performance by the groups will require them to engage in a high level of intragroup dialogue.
  Group answers and responses can be displayed easily and quickly.
- Use assignments that are characterized by the 4 S's:
  Significant problem. Individuals or groups should work on a problem that is significant to students.
  Same problem. Individuals or groups should work on the same problem, case, or question.
  Specific choice. Individuals or groups should be required to use course concepts to make a specific choice.
  Simultaneous report. Whenever possible individuals and groups should report their choices simultaneously.
- Having groups write a term paper or any other kind of lengthy document is not a good group assignment. Creating lengthy documents seldom promotes a high level of discussion within or between groups.

Activity 5: Provide feedback that helps the groups and individuals learn

- The feedback on the application exercises should be frequent and immediate.
- The feedback should come in a form that allows the individuals to see what was good about their response and what could have been better. Usually this can be accomplished by allowing them to compare their response with the responses of other groups, as well as occasionally getting an assessment from the teacher.

End of the Course

Activity 6: Culminating project

- The culminating project for a two- to three-week unit (or for the whole course) should integrate as much of the course content as possible. Hence, it should be a complex, challenging task characterized by the 4 S's.
- This will generally be a graded project, so the teacher needs to determine how to distinguish poor, mediocre, and excellent responses. Sometimes a valuable learning activity is to have the class develop the assessment criteria before they start working on the project.

Activity 7: Peer evaluation

- At the end of the course, each student completes an evaluation of the other members of their team. This evaluation needs to be set up so that it elicits a peer evaluation score for each student's course grade.
- The criteria for the peer evaluation can be provided by the teacher or generated by the class or by each team.

- The evaluation should have a numerical component accompanied by a brief narrative statement for each student.
- Some teachers find it valuable to do a peer evaluation in the middle of the course. The results are provided to students but not recorded in the grade book.

There are three types of valuable resources for learning how to do each of these tasks:

- Books: *Team-Based Learning: A Transformative Use of Small Groups in College Teaching,* by L. K. Michaelsen, A. B. Knight, and L. D. Fink (Sterling, Va.: Stylus, 2004), and *Team-Based Learning in Health Professions Education,* by L. K. Michaelsen, D. X. Parmelee, K. K. McMahon, and R. E. Levine (Sterling, Va.: Stylus, 2008).
- Web sites: www.teambasedlearning.org (the official TBL site), www.tlcollaborative.org (a site for health professions educators), and http://cis.apsc.ubc.ca/wiki/index.php/Team-Based_Learning (a site for engineering educators). Each site has multiple subsections, many with valuable resources for educators from any discipline.
- TBL Listserv: Anyone can sign up for this listserv from the www.teambasedlearning.org main page. It currently has approximately two hundred people, 20 percent of whom live outside the United States. It usually has an active dialogue when people pose questions.

INDEX

NEW DIRECTIONS FOR TEACHING AND LEARNING

ORDER FORM SUBSCRIPTION AND SINGLE ISSUES

DISCOUNTED BACK ISSUES:

Use this form to receive 20% off all back issues of *New Directions for Teaching and Learning*.
All single issues priced at **$23.20** (normally $29.00)

TITLE	ISSUE NO.	ISBN
_____	_____	_____
_____	_____	_____
_____	_____	_____

*Call 888-378-2537 or see mailing instructions below. When calling, mention the promotional code JB9ND
to receive your discount. For a complete list of issues, please visit www.josseybass.com/go/ndtl*

SUBSCRIPTIONS: (1 YEAR, 4 ISSUES)

☐ New Order   ☐ Renewal

U.S.	☐ Individual: $89	☐ Institutional: $228
CANADA/MEXICO	☐ Individual: $89	☐ Institutional: $268
ALL OTHERS	☐ Individual: $113	☐ Institutional: $302

*Call 888-378-2537 or see mailing and pricing instructions below.
Online subscriptions are available at www.interscience.wiley.com*

ORDER TOTALS:

Issue / Subscription Amount: $ _____

Shipping Amount: $ _____
(for single issues only – subscription prices include shipping)

Total Amount: $ _____

SHIPPING CHARGES:	
First Item	$5.00
Each Add'l Item	$3.00

*(No sales tax for U.S. subscriptions. Canadian residents, add GST for subscription orders. Individual rate subscriptions must
be paid by personal check or credit card. Individual rate subscriptions may not be resold as library copies.)*

BILLING & SHIPPING INFORMATION:

☐ **PAYMENT ENCLOSED:** *(U.S. check or money order only. All payments must be in U.S. dollars.)*

☐ **CREDIT CARD:** ☐ VISA ☐ MC ☐ AMEX

Card number _____ Exp. Date_____

Card Holder Name_____ Card Issue # _____

Signature _____ Day Phone_____

☐ **BILL ME:** *(U.S. institutional orders only. Purchase order required.)*

Purchase order # _____
Federal Tax ID 13559302 • GST 89102-8052

Name_____

Address_____

Phone_____ E-mail_____

Copy or detach page and send to: **John Wiley & Sons, PTSC, 5th Floor
989 Market Street, San Francisco, CA 94103-1741**

Order Form can also be faxed to: **888-481-2665**

PROMO JB9ND